AS Economics
UNIT 2
2ND EDITION

AQA

Module 2: The National Economy

Ray Powell

To Christine

Philip Allan Updates
Market Place
Deddington
Oxfordshire
OX15 0SE

Orders
Bookpoint Ltd, 130 Milton Park, Abingdon, Oxfordshire, OX14 4SB
tel: 01235 827720
fax: 01235 400454
e-mail: uk.orders@bookpoint.co.uk
Lines are open 9.00 a.m.–5.00 p.m., Monday to Saturday, with a 24-hour message answering service. You can also order through the Philip Allan Updates website: www.philipallan.co.uk

ISBN 978-0-86003-895-5

This Guide has been written specifically to support students preparing for the AQA AS Economics Unit 2 examination. The content has been neither approved nor endorsed by AQA and remains the sole responsibility of the author.

Printed by MPG Books, Bodmin

Philip Allan Updates' policy is to use papers that are natural, renewable and recyclable products and made from wood grown in sustainable forests. The logging and manufacturing processes are expected to conform to the environmental regulations of the country of origin.

Contents

Introduction

■ ■ ■

Content Guidance

■ ■ ■

Questions and Answers

Introduction

The aim of this guide is to prepare students for the AQA Advanced Subsidiary Unit 2 examination assessing Module 2: The National Economy. You should use the guide as follows:

(1) Read the introduction.

(2) The second and third sections of the book should then be used as supplements to other resources, such as class notes, textbooks, *Economic Review* magazine and *AS/A-Level Economics Revision Notes*. (The last two of these are published by Philip Allan Updates.) Because it contains summaries rather than in-depth coverage of all the topics in the specification, you should not use the guide as your sole learning resource during the main part of the course. You are strongly advised to make full use of the Question and Answer section, especially in the revision period when you should be concentrating on improving your examination skills.

Examinable skills

The Unit examination is 1 hour long, has a maximum mark of 40 and contains two question papers, both of which must be answered. Paper ECN2/1, which accounts for 15 marks (approximately 37% of the total), comprises 15 compulsory objective test questions, which in this guide are called **multiple-choice questions** (MCQs). One mark will be awarded for each MCQ answered correctly. Paper ECN2/2 accounts for 25 marks (approximately 63% of the total) and comprises two **data-response questions** (DRQs) of which you should answer one.

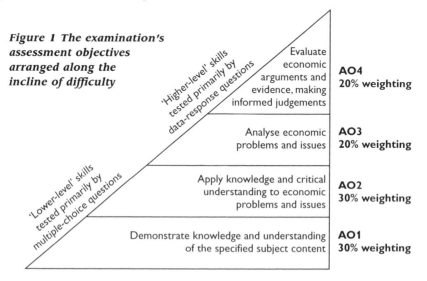

Figure 1 The examination's assessment objectives arranged along the incline of difficulty

'Higher-level' skills tested primarily by data-response questions

'Lower-level' skills tested primarily by multiple-choice questions

Evaluate economic arguments and evidence, making informed judgements	**AO4** 20% weighting
Analyse economic problems and issues	**AO3** 20% weighting
Apply knowledge and critical understanding to economic problems and issues	**AO2** 30% weighting
Demonstrate knowledge and understanding of the specified subject content	**AO1** 30% weighting

The examination has four **assessment objectives** (AOs), as shown in Figure 1, together with their examination weightings, arranged in an incline of difficulty. Lower-level skills of knowledge and factual-recall are included in AO1 (at the bottom of the incline). Moving up the incline, increasingly higher-level skills feature in the AOs: application of knowledge and critical understanding (AO2); analysis of problems (AO3); evaluation of arguments and evidence (AO4). Overall, 60% of the examination questions are knowledge-based, testing the relatively lower-level skills in AOs 1 and 2. The remaining 40% of examination questions meet AOs 3 and 4.

Multiple-choice skills

Each multiple-choice question contains a stem followed by four possible answers (A, B, C and D), only one of which is correct. Typically MCQs are set to test candidates' ability to perform simple calculations and their knowledge of key definitions and concepts, especially on parts of the specification not covered by the data-response questions. MCQs primarily test the lower-level skills related to knowledge and understanding in AOs 1 and 2. You should expect six of the 15 MCQs to test AO1, a further five to test AO2, and the remaining four to test AO3, the analysis of economic problems and issues. AO4 is not tested in the multiple-choice question section of the examination paper.

Data-response skills

Whereas the 15 MCQs in Paper ECN2/1 of the examination paper are compulsory, Paper ECN2/2 comprises two data-response questions of which you must answer one. The DRQs are numbered **Question 1** and **2**. Each question contains three sub-questions, listed as (a), (b) and (c). The mark allocation is (a) 4 marks, (b) 6 marks, (c) 15 marks.

The layout and structure of the questions will be similar to the six data-response questions included in the Question and Answer section of this guide. Each question is likely to contain two or three sets of data, usually extracted from different original sources, such as newspaper or magazine articles. When three data sets are used in both questions, they will be labelled **Extract A**, **Extract B** and **Extract C** for Question 1, and **Extract D**, **Extract E** and **Extract F** for Question 2. In each question, one set of data is likely to be numerical, for example a line graph, a bar graph, a pie graph or a table. Text or passage data will almost always be extracted or adapted from original sources, with the original source indicated. Numerical data will generally be taken from original sources, but there may be exceptions.

Both DRQs will be structured in exactly the same way and test the same assessment objectives. The questions are supposed to be equally difficult, but in practice almost every student finds one question more attractive than the other. Whichever question you initially favour, don't rush your choice of question. Careful thought and a sensible final decision are necessary if you are to do yourself full justice. You don't want to realise 10 minutes into your answer that you can't answer part (c) and that it is too late to switch questions.

An 'incline of difficulty' will always be built into the DRQs, with the earlier parts of each question being the most straightforward. The first two parts of each DRQ will be marked using an **issue-based mark scheme** which lists the marks that can be awarded for the particular issues (and associated development) that might be included in the answer.

The last part of each DRQ differs from the earlier parts in three significant ways. First, and most obvious, the last part of the question carries many more marks than the earlier three parts — 60% of the total marks for the question and 37% for the whole paper. If you time the examination incorrectly and fail to develop your answer to part (c) beyond a cursory footnote, you will reduce considerably your chance of achieving grade A. Second, whereas questions (a) and (b) should be answered quite briefly, you are expected to write an extended answer of several paragraphs for part (c). You should think of this as a 'mini' essay. Third, 'higher-level' skills are expected. Because of this, a completely different type of mark scheme, known as a **levels of response mark scheme**, is used for the last part of each DRQ. It is vital for you to familiarise yourself with this mark scheme and to bear it in mind when you practise data-response questions.

The first two parts of each DRQ test primarily the lower-level skills of AOs 1 and 2, whereas the final part, which carries the most marks, tests primarily the higher-level skills set out in AOs 3 and 4. Part (a) of each question will probably relate to the numerical data. You are likely to be asked to describe the main changes in the data, or to compare the changes in two data series.

The second part of each DRQ, part (b), is likely to include the key instruction to 'explain'. This question is about causes of events taking place in the data. It tests whether you can use basic economic theory and analysis in a clear and reasoned way to cast light on an issue. When answering such a question, a golden rule is: *Simple theories used well are always preferable to convoluted and difficult theoretical explanation obviously misunderstood.* Sometimes the question might include the following instruction: 'With the help of a diagram, explain...' But even if the question does not contain an explicit instruction to include a diagram, *relevant* and *accurate* diagrams could improve your answer.

Part (c) carries significantly more marks and therefore requires a longer and more developed answer than parts (a) and (b). Whereas the earlier parts of the question are firmly based on describing and explaining elements of the data, you should expect the last part of the question to veer away from the data. An example of the wording you should expect a part (c) question to take is:

Identify and evaluate the possible effects on (some aspect of the wider economy) of (one or more of the events described in the data). You might also be asked to: **Justify your reasoning**.

Most importantly, a key command word to '**discuss**', '**assess**' or '**evaluate**' must be obeyed for your answer to reach the higher Level 3 and Level 4 standards of attainment set out in the levels of response mark scheme. Part (c) is the only part of the whole examination paper set specifically to meet assessment objective 4:

evaluation of arguments and evidence, and the *making of informed judgements*. Your answer *must* evaluate the different arguments you set out in your answer to part (c). With many questions, discussion should centre on evaluating the advantages and disadvantages of, or costs and benefits of, or the 'case for' versus the 'case against', a course of action mentioned in the question.

Finally, always try to finish your answer with a conclusion, the nature of which should vary according to the type of discussion or evaluation required. The conclusion might judge the relative strengths of the arguments discussed, possibly highlighting the most important argument. With many questions it is more appropriate to conclude whether, on balance, the 'case for' is stronger than the 'case against' and to provide some justification for your opinion.

Even if your conclusion sits on the fence, saying little more than 'it all depends on circumstances', it can earn marks in two different ways. First, a conclusion, which justifies your opinion, provides the examiner marking your script with evidence of evaluation — the skill needed for your answer to reach a Level 3 or 4 standard. Second, the mark band descriptors that are used for assessing part (c) of each DRQ incorporate statements that relate to the quality of written communication in your answer. To earn maximum marks for this, your answer to part (c) must be well organised and this requires a suitable conclusion.

The mark scheme also instructs the examiner marking your paper to assess quality of written communication when applying the issue-based mark scheme to parts (a) and (b) of your answer. When deciding how many marks to award for the development of any point made, the examiner must take account of:
- use of appropriate format and style of writing to organise relevant information clearly and coherently
- use of specialist vocabulary, where appropriate
- legibility of handwriting
- accuracy of spelling, punctuation and grammar

A strategy for tackling the examination

(1) On opening the examination booklet, turn immediately to Section B and spend up to 5 minutes reading *both* DRQs.
(2) Then go back to Section A and spend up to 17 minutes answering the 15 MCQs, completing your first run through the questions. While you are doing this, you will be thinking subconsciously about the DRQs.
(3) Read through both DRQs again, paying particular attention to whether you can write a good answer to part (c) of each question, the part that carries the most marks.
(4) After careful thought, make your final choice and spend about 35 minutes answering *all* the parts of the DRQ. Take account of the marks indicated in brackets for each sub-question when allocating the 35 minutes between each part of the question. Make sure you spend over half the time answering part (c).
(5) In the last 8 minutes of the examination, complete a second run through the MCQs

and read through your written answers to check for and correct mistakes, including spelling and grammatical mistakes.

Revision planning

Once you have completed your course of study, the most daunting task still remains to be faced: to do yourself justice when presented with unseen questions amid the stresses and strains of the examination room.

If you have studied diligently and if you use this guide wisely, particularly in the weeks leading up to the examination, you should achieve the grade of which you are capable. You can reduce the need for luck by preparing and then following a revision programme. Begin your revision planning several weeks before the examination, timetabling periods of each day when you know you can work for at least an hour completely free of distraction. Allow yourself a brief relaxation period every half-hour or so to facilitate the absorption of what you have revised intensively in the previous period. Although you must cover the whole specification (to enable you to answer all the MCQs), concentrate on key concepts and essential economic theory rather than on descriptive fact and historical detail.

The revision strategy below is based on the use of this guide, supplemented by other resources such as the notes you have built up over your course of study, and favoured textbooks. The programme is designed for the 3-week period before the examination. The strategy assumes you are revising at least three other AS subjects during the same 3-week period, but are able to devote a session of 2 hours (plus half an hour for short breaks) to economics every other day, with shorter follow-up sessions on the intervening days. You should revise solidly for 6 days a week, but allow yourself a day off a week to recharge your batteries. The strategy can be modified to meet your personal needs and preferences, for example by shortening each revision session and/or extending the sessions over a revision period longer than 3 weeks.

(1) Revise one topic from the Content Guidance section of this guide per revision session. Divide the revision session into four half-hour periods during which you are working solidly and without distraction, interspersed with 10-minute breaks.
(2) Proceed through the topics in the order they appear in the guide:
    Week 1: 1–3
    Week 2: 4–6
    Week 3: 7–9
(3) Vary the activities you undertake in each 30-minute period of a revision session. For example, spend the first 30 minutes reading through the 'Essential information' section at the beginning of each topic in this book. List key terms and concepts on a piece of paper. After a short break, use the second 30-minute period to check more fully the meaning of the key terms and concepts in your class notes and/or an economics textbook. Then, after a second short break, check which multiple-choice questions and parts of data-response questions in the Question and Answer section of the guide test aspects of the topic you are revising. Spend the rest of the 30 minutes

answering some or all of the questions. In the final 30-minute period (or perhaps in a follow-up session a day or two later), carefully read through the examiner's comments on the MCQs and the student's answers and examiner's comments on the DRQs covered by the topic.

(4) To vary your revision programme (and to make sure you reinforce and retain the vital information revised in the longer sessions), fit some of the activities suggested below into follow-up sessions. Normally you should plan at least a single half-hour follow-up session for each day between your long session days. Be prepared also to undertake unplanned 10-minute sessions whenever you find yourself with a few spare minutes, for example when waiting for a meal or for a television programme to start. Activities suitable for follow-up and 10-minute sessions include the following:

- **Write definitions** of some of the key terms and concepts relating to the topic revised on the previous day. Check each of your definitions against the correct definition in this guide, in a textbook or in your class notes.
- **Draw** key diagrams relating to the topic. Check any diagram you draw against a correct version of the diagram, making absolutely sure that the diagram is correctly and clearly labelled.
- Whenever you make mistakes, **repeat these exercises** every day or so, until you have eliminated all the mistakes.
- **Answer questions** from past AQA examination papers and from AQA's 'Specimen Units and Mark Schemes' booklet, which your teacher should have. Make sure your teacher obtains all the relevant AQA past exam papers that are available at the time you take the examination. Identify and then answer questions from past papers that relate to the topic just revised. Then spend another follow-up session checking your answer(s) against the AQA mark scheme(s) to see how you could improve.

Note: if you wish to buy copies of past examination papers and mark schemes, contact: The Publications Department, The Assessment and Qualifications Alliance, Aldon House, 39 Heald Grove, Manchester M14 4NA (tel. 0161 953 1170).

Content
Guidance

The **National Economy** module is concerned with **macroeconomics**. Whereas microeconomics studies 'the little bits' of the economy, macroeconomics looks at the **whole economy**. It investigates issues such as what determines the aggregate levels of **employment** and **unemployment** in the economy, the **price level** and its rate of growth (**inflation**), and the value of the **trade flows** into and out of the economy (the **balance of payments**).

The national economy referred to in the title of the module is the **United Kingdom economy**. According to the specification (or syllabus), you should have a **good knowledge of trends and developments in the UK economy and of government policies during the 10 years before the examination**. Awareness of earlier events may be useful, but will not be tested in the examination. The examination will require you to apply economic theory and your knowledge of events taking place in the economy, and to assess the effectiveness of current and recent government policies. In particular, you must analyse economic problems and policy using the **aggregate demand/aggregate supply (AD/AS) macroeconomic model**. You must also be aware that the performance of the UK economy is influenced by external events in the international economy, and in particular by membership of the **European Union (EU)**. Last, but not least, you must be familiar with various forms of data and statistics used for presenting information about the national economy.

The introduction to the specification which follows (pp. 13–15) contains a summary of the AQA specification for Module 2: The National Economy. This is followed by more detail about each section of the specification under the following headings:

- National income and economic growth (p. 16)
- Policy objectives and conflicts (p. 19)
- Employment, unemployment and inflation (p. 22)
- Aggregate demand (p. 25)
- The AD/AS macroeconomic model (p. 28)
- Fiscal policy (p. 32)
- Monetary policy (p. 35)
- Supply-side policies (p. 38)
- National economic performance (p. 41)

Handwritten annotations:

CPI = Consumer Price index

↳ Basket of goods.
Av. Households.
(750)
↳ Prices measured across UK.

Index No.   100 BASE YR

100   '05   ∴ ↑ 10 %.
110   '06

· Eco growth
· Full employment
· low/stable inflation
· BoP.

$\frac{P\Delta X \times \omega}{\varepsilon \omega}$ = Index Fig.

· Equity   Regressive
Lo proportion ↑ as ~

↑ % Tax as Y ↑ i.e income tax.

2 successive $\frac{1}{4}$'s of -ve growth.

Introduction to the specification

The AQA specification for the National Economy contains the following sections:

11.1 Performance of the UK economy and government policy objectives

To gain a confident understanding of macroeconomics and the national economy, you must be able to distinguish between the **objectives and instruments of economic policy**. Policy objectives (which form an important part of section 11.1) are targets or goals that the government wishes to achieve or hit. By contrast, policy instruments are the means governments use to try to achieve their objectives. (These policy instruments form the subject matter of section 11.3.)

At all times you should remember that the ultimate purpose of government policy is to **improve economic welfare**. More narrowly, the specification requires knowledge and understanding of four objectives of government macroeconomic policy. These are: **full employment** (or **low unemployment**); **economic growth** (and **higher living standards**); **control of inflation**; and a **satisfactory balance of payments**. Unlike the first three which are **internal policy objectives** relating to the domestic economy, the fourth is an **external objective** that involves the UK's relations with the rest of the world. In recent years, the external objective has tended to be stated in terms of **achieving or supporting a particular exchange rate** rather than in terms of the balance of payments. (In this guide, reference is also made to a fifth policy objective: a **fair or equitable distribution of income and wealth**.)

If all five objectives could be achieved simultaneously all the time, the economic problem would largely disappear. However, it is very difficult and perhaps impossible to achieve this. Very often, the more successful a government is at hitting one particular objective, the poorer is its performance with regard to one or more of the other objectives. Governments are often faced with **policy conflicts**, which they may try to resolve by **trading off** between competing objectives. (A trade-off occurs when a government tries to achieve an acceptable level of performance with regard to two competing objectives because it is difficult and perhaps impossible to achieve both fully at the same time. For example, the government might aim for a 4% unemployment rate and a 2.5% inflation rate because it believes that absolute full employment and zero inflation are mutually exclusive and impossible to achieve together.)

As well as objectives and instruments, there are also performance and policy indicators. A **performance indicator** enables you to compare the economic performance of the UK economy with that of other countries. Occasionally, a data-response question in the examination may include data for four or five countries on performance indicators such as comparative economic growth rates, employment and unemployment statistics, inflation rates and trade balances. (By contrast to a performance indicator, a **policy indicator** provides information as to whether a particular aspect of macroeconomic policy is on course to achieve its objective. For example, data on the **money supply** is used to **indicate** the tightness or looseness of **monetary policy**. Too fast a rate of growth of the money supply might indicate that the main **monetary policy instrument** (the **rate of interest**) should be raised to enable the **monetary policy objective** (**control of inflation**) to be achieved.

11.2 How the macroeconomy works

This is the theoretical core of the specification, and centres on the **aggregate demand/aggregate supply (AD/AS) macroeconomic model** of the economy.

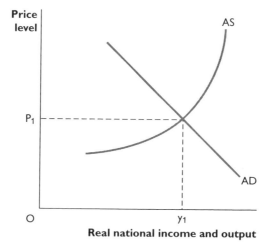

Figure 1 A simple aggregate demand/ aggregate supply (AD/AS) macroeconomic model

Aggregate demand in the economy represents the total expenditure upon national output that all the economic agents in the economy wish to undertake. It comprises **consumption** spending by households, **investment** spending by firms, **government spending** and the net amount spent on the economy's output by the rest of the world (spending on **exports** minus spending by UK residents on **imports**). In much the same way, **aggregate supply** represents the total output of goods and services which all the firms or producers in the economy wish to supply or sell.

The availability and **quality of factors of production** (e.g. capital, labour and the state of technology) determine **aggregate supply**. It is also determined by the impact of **institutional and cultural factors** such as the existence of an **entrepreneurial culture** and appropriate **incentives** for taking risks and supplying labour.

The AD curve in Figure 1 shows that aggregate demand for output increases the lower the price level. By contrast, the AS curve shows that the aggregate supply of output increases at higher price levels. **Macroeconomic equilibrium** occurs in the national economy at the level of real national income or output at which the total planned expenditure upon output equals the quantity of goods and services firms are willing and able to supply, i.e. at the level of output at which **AD = AS**. In Figure 1, macro-economic equilibrium occurs at the level of output y_1.

The AS curve in Figure 1 is a **short-run aggregate supply curve**, which you must not confuse with a **long-run aggregate supply curve**. Whereas short-run AS curves slope upward, the long-run AS curve is always vertical. By contrast to the short run (which is when firms respond to price increases by supplying more output), supply does not respond to an increase in prices in the long run. It is important to understand this distinction and the resulting implications for economic policy. (An LRAS curve is illustrated in Figure 8 on p. 30 and Figure 9 on p. 39.)

11.3 The main instruments of government macroeconomic policy

Whereas specification section 11.1 covers the objectives of macroeconomic policy, this section is concerned with the types of economic policy, or policy instruments, used to try to achieve the objectives. This involves **fiscal policy**, **monetary policy** and **supply-side policies**. You must understand the broad meaning of all three and the particular policy instruments involved.

Fiscal policy covers **taxation** and **government spending** and the government's **budget deficit** or **surplus**, while **interest rates** are the main monetary policy instrument. In the past, fiscal policy was mostly used to influence aggregate demand, but nowadays it is aimed more at the supply-side of the economy than at the demand-side, and at maintaining **macroeconomic stability**.

In **monetary policy**, interest rates are raised or lowered primarily to manage aggregate demand in pursuit of the objective of controlling inflation. The specification also requires you to understand how monetary policy may affect the money supply and the exchange rate, and the role of the Bank of England in implementing monetary policy.

It is now generally agreed that the success of the UK economy depends on how well the supply-side of the economy performs. Consequently, much emphasis is now placed on **supply-side policy**. Supply-side policies are those free-market and anti-interventionist government policies that increase the economy's production potential by improving competition and the efficiency of markets and resource allocation.

Finally, you must use the AD/AS macroeconomic model (the core of specification section 11.2) to illustrate, analyse and evaluate the effects of monetary, fiscal and supply-side policies. Because monetary policy is used to influence aggregate demand in the national economy, its main effect is to shift the AD curve rightwards or leftwards. (In the long-run, however, successful monetary policy can contribute to the rightward-shift of the long-run AS curve by achieving low and stable inflation.) Supply-side policies are used to shift the long-run AS curve rightwards. As noted, fiscal policy *can* be used to shift the AD curve, but these days it is used primarily as a supply-side policy to promote the rightward-shift of aggregate supply.

National income and economic growth

These notes relate to AQA specification section 11.1 and prepare you to answer AQA examination questions on two key macroeconomic topics relating to the national economy:
- national income
- economic growth

Essential information

You must remember that the main purpose of economic activity is to improve economic welfare and people's standards of living. For the most part, this requires increased levels of consumption of material goods and services, which in turn requires the economy to produce higher levels of output or **national income**.

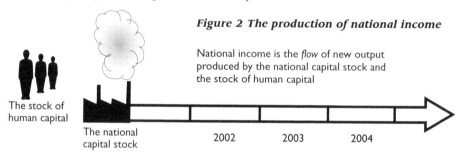

Figure 2 The production of national income

National income is the *flow* of new output produced by the national capital stock and the stock of human capital

The stock of human capital

The national capital stock   2002   2003   2004

To understand national income, you must appreciate the difference between **stocks** and **flows**. There is always a **national capital stock** (the *stock* of natural resources and capital goods accumulated from previous production) and a **stock of human capital** (the skills of the working population). These are depicted by the symbols in the left-hand part of Figure 2. National income (shown by the arrow in Figure 2) is the *flow* of new output **produced** in a particular period (for example 2003) by combining the economy's stocks of physical and human capital.

This flow of new output can be measured in three ways. When measured as the output produced by the economy, it is often called **national product**. It can also be measured by the incomes paid to the owners of the capital and labour (and other factors of production) that produce the output. Finally, it can be measured by the expenditure of these incomes upon the output. Since these are simply three different ways of measuring the same flow of new output, it follows that:

national output = national income = national expenditure
(or national product)

You must appreciate that economists use the terms income and output interchangeably. National income, national output and national product have exactly the same meaning. Don't, however, confuse *real* national income and *money* national income. **Real national income** or output refers to the actual goods and services produced by the economy, measured in physical units such the quantity of cars or financial services produced. By contrast, **money national income** (or **nominal national income**) measures this output in monetary terms at the price level when the output was produced. The relationship between money national income and real national income is:

money national income = real national income × the price level

The arrow in Figure 2 shows the *flow* of national income over three years: 2002, 2003 and 2004. When producing national income in a particular year (2003 for example), part of the national capital stock wears out. Unless worn out capital is replaced, the national capital stock shrinks and **negative economic growth** occurs. To prevent this, part of 2003's national income must be **invested** to repair or make good the size of the capital stock. **Gross national product (GNP)** refers to national income *before* deducting the amount of income invested to maintain the capital stock. **Net national product (NNP)** measures national income or output after this payment has been made. Although the specification does not require knowledge of this distinction, GNP data may appear in examination questions, as may another national income term, **gross domestic product (GDP)**. GDP is similar to GNP, but measures the flow of output produced *within* the UK. By contrast, GNP adds in profits flowing to UK companies from their activities overseas, while deducting profits flowing out of the UK made by overseas multinational companies.

Economic growth, which is usually *measured* by the percentage annual increase in real national income, can be *defined* as an **increase in the economy's productive potential**. A **production possibility diagram** such as Figure 3 can be used to illustrate economic growth.

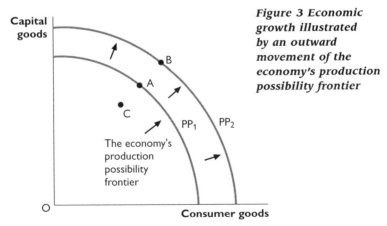

Figure 3 Economic growth illustrated by an outward movement of the economy's production possibility frontier

A production possibility frontier such as PP_1 shows all the possible combinations of capital goods and consumer goods that the economy could produce if using available stocks of physical and human capital to the full. All points on the frontier, such as point A, depict **full employment**, whereas **unemployment** occurs at all points inside the frontier such as point C. When the economy is on the frontier at A, it is impossible to produce more consumer goods without reducing production of capital goods — unless economic growth takes place. The outward movement of the economy's production possibility frontier shows economic growth, for example from PP_1 to PP_2.

A number of factors contribute to economic growth, including **higher labour productivity, technical progress**, **growth of the working population** and **investment** to improve the quality of **human capital**. Economic growth generally requires the stock of physical capital (or capital goods) to grow in size and for its quality to improve. Part of the current flow of output must be used to replace worn out capital goods and there must be further **investment to enlarge and improve the capital stock**.

Examination skills

The skills most likely to be tested by multiple-choice and data-response questions on national income and economic growth are as follows:

- Interpreting and analysing GNP or GDP tables for a number of countries to compare levels of output and growth rates.
- Understanding the differences between money and real national income, and their rates of growth.
- Defining economic growth and illustrating it on a production possibility diagram such as Figure 3.
- Distinguishing between a particular year's growth rate and the trend rate of growth.
- Relating the level of national income and economic growth to the business cycle.
- Explaining conflicts between economic growth and other objectives of government macroeconomic policy.

Examination questions

You should expect up to three multiple-choice questions on the terms and concepts listed in specification section 11.1 on this topic. Of the questions included in the Question and Answer section of this guide, MCQs 1 and 2 (in both Tests 1 and 2) provide typical examples. You should answer these questions either now or in your revision programme, and then read carefully the examiner's comments for each question. DRQ 5 covers the relationship between economic growth and productivity, while DRQ 1 tests understanding of issues relating to the UK's trend rate of growth and possible structural change occurring in the UK economy.

Common examination errors

Commonly made mistakes on national income and economic growth include the following:

- Failure to appreciate that national income and national output are the same.
- Confusing money and real national income.
- Inaccurate drawing of production possibility diagrams to illustrate economic growth.
- Asserting that growth is always beneficial and has no costs or disadvantages.

- Confusing the measured growth rate for a particular year with the underlying trend rate of growth.
- Failure to appreciate the role of factors such as investment, technical progress and quality of human capital in promoting economic growth.

Policy objectives and conflicts

These notes relate to AQA specification section 11.1 and prepare you to answer AQA examination questions on:

- the objectives of government macroeconomic policy
- conflicts between policy objectives

Essential information

In pursuit of the **ultimate objective** of economic policy, namely **improved economic welfare** for all the population, it is usual to identify five principal objectives of government macroeconomic policy. These are:

(1) Full employment (or **low unemployment**).

(2) Economic growth (and **higher living standards**).

(3) A fair or **equitable distribution of income and wealth**.

(4) Control of inflation (or **price stability**).

(5) External policy objectives such as a satisfactory **balance of payments** or a particular **exchange rate target**.

The order of the list above represents a **Keynesian** ranking of macroeconomic policy objectives. (In the three decades following the First World War, John Maynard Keynes was the British economist most responsible for creating macroeconomic theory and policy.) Keynesian economics is generally associated with the use of **demand management policies** to try to achieve full employment and economic growth. To achieve these objectives, the government **reflates** the economy by injecting demand into the economy. In the past, both **monetary policy** and **fiscal policy** were used for this purpose, though in recent years only monetary policy has been used. Expansionary or reflationary monetary policy involves cutting interest rates. (When fiscal policy is used for this purpose, there are tax cuts and increases in government spending.) However, as the economy approaches full employment, the expansion of demand tends to draw in too many imports and/or to increase inflation. These problems may force the government to reverse policy in order to reduce the level of aggregate demand. **Deflationary policies**, such as increased interest rates (monetary policy), public spending cuts and increased taxes (fiscal policy) can be used to reduce inflationary pressures or to improve the balance of payments.

Although monetary policy is now used to manage the level of demand in the economy, UK macroeconomic policy is no longer really Keynesian. In the early 1980s, macroeconomic policy was **monetarist**. Monetarists believe that inflation is caused by an excessive rate of growth of the **money supply** (or stock on money in the economy). Monetarist economists believe that to control inflation, the rate of growth in the money supply must first be controlled. While Keynesians generally regard full employment and economic growth as the principal policy objectives, monetarists make control of inflation the priority. They believe that competitive markets and entrepreneurship (as opposed to governments) create full employment and that governments should be **enablers** rather than **providers**. Monetarists maintain that the function of government is to foster the conditions in which competitive and efficient markets can create jobs and produce growth. One of these conditions is low inflation, which monetarists believe should be the principal objective of macroeconomic policy.

These days the term 'monetarism' is not as fashionable as it used to be, largely because less attention is given to the role of the money supply in causing inflation. The terms '**free-market**' and '**supply-side**' macroeconomics have tended to replace monetarism. Free-market or supply-side economics encompasses monetarism, but emphasises the role of free markets in achieving a healthy and competitive national economy. Emphasis is also given to the need to reduce rather than to increase the size and role of government in the economy by **deregulation** and **privatisation**. Free-market economists have continued to support the monetarist belief that governments should actively use monetary policy to control inflation.

Because of the difficulty of achieving all five macroeconomic objectives at the same time, policy-makers have often settled for the lesser goal of **trading-off** between conflicting aims. A **conflict** exists when two or more desirable objectives are mutually exclusive. The government attempts to resolve this conflict by a trade-off between competing objectives. This may involve achieving a relatively satisfactory performance with regard to two conflicting objectives, or it may mean switching periodically from one objective to another, e.g. accepting higher unemployment and lower growth (for a time) in order to reduce inflation or improve the balance of payments.

Over the years, UK macroeconomic policy has been influenced and constrained by three significant policy conflicts and trade-offs. These have been:
(1) The conflict between the **internal policy objectives** of full employment and growth and the **external objective** of achieving a satisfactory balance of payments (or possibly supporting a particular exchange rate). From 1990 to 1992, this trade-off was significant while the exchange rate of the pound was fixed within the **exchange rate mechanism (ERM)** of the **European Monetary System (EMS)**. It could become significant again if a UK government decides it must achieve and maintain a particular exchange rate as a necessary condition for replacing the pound with the **EU single currency**, the **euro**.

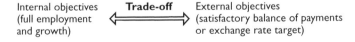

Internal objectives (full employment and growth)   **Trade-off**   External objectives (satisfactory balance of payments or exchange rate target)

(2) The conflict between **full employment** and **control of inflation**. This is often called the **Phillips curve** trade-off.

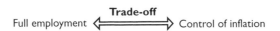

Trade-off

Full employment ⟺ Control of inflation

(3) The conflict between **economic growth** and a **more equal distribution of income and wealth**. During the Keynesian era, **progressive taxation** and **transfers** to the poor were used (as part of fiscal policy) to reduce inequalities between rich and poor. In recent years, free-market supply-side economists have argued that such policies reduce entrepreneurial and personal incentives in the labour market, inhibit growth and make the economy less competitive. In the free-market view, greater inequalities may be necessary to create the labour and entrepreneurial incentives deemed necessary for rapid and sustainable economic growth.

Trade-off

Greater equality ⟺ Faster economic growth

Examination skills

The skills most likely to be tested by multiple-choice and data-response questions on policy objectives and conflicts are as follows:

- Identifying and briefly explaining the meaning of the objectives of macroeconomic policy.
- Understanding the importance of different policy objectives in recent years.
- Comparing the performance of the UK and other countries in achieving policy objectives.
- Explaining how different policy instruments (monetary, fiscal and supply-side) are used to achieve particular objectives.
- Analysing policy to achieve objectives by using the AD/AS macroeconomic model.
- Explaining conflicts between competing policy objectives.
- Applying the concept of a trade-off to analyse and evaluate governments' attempts to resolve policy conflicts.

Examination questions

You should expect up to two multiple-choice questions on the terms and concepts listed in specification section 11.1 on this topic. Of the questions included in the Question and Answer section of this guide, MCQs 4 and 5 in Test 1 and 3 in Test 2 provide typical examples. DRQ 4 covers the conflict between employment and inflation, while DRQ 6 touches upon the conflict between the pursuit of internal objectives and the external objective of maintaining a satisfactory balance of payments.

Common examination errors

Commonly made mistakes on policy objectives and conflicts include:

- Failure to explain the meaning of particular policy objectives such as full employment.
- Confusing policy objectives, policy instruments, and policy and performance indicators.

- Failure to explain sufficiently particular conflicts between policy objectives.
- Failure to appreciate how the nature of policy objectives and conflicts has changed over the years.
- Inability to make relevant comparisons with other countries.

Employment, unemployment and inflation

These notes relate to AQA specification section 11.1 and prepare you to answer AQA examination questions on two key macroeconomic topics:
- employment and unemployment
- inflation

Essential information

Free-market economists define **full employment** in terms of the **aggregate demand for** and the **aggregate supply of** labour in the economy, as illustrated in Figure 4. The downward-sloping aggregate demand curve for labour shows that as the **real wage** rate paid to workers falls, employers or entrepreneurs are willing to employ more labour. The aggregate supply curve of labour is upward sloping, showing that workers are prepared to supply more labour as the real wage rate rises. Full employment occurs at the market-clearing real wage rate at which the number of workers wishing to work equals the number of workers employers wish to hire.

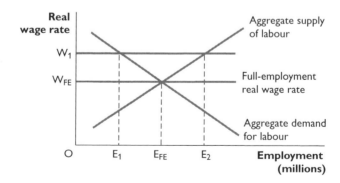

Figure 4 Full employment illustrated in the economy's aggregate labour market

Full employment does not necessarily mean that every single member of the working population is in work. Rather, it is when **the number of people wishing to work at the going market wage equals the number of workers employers wish to hire at this wage**. In Figure 4 this is shown at the level of employment E_{FE}, at the real wage rate of W_{FE}.

Suppose, however, that the actual real wage rate in the labour market is above w_{FE}, for example at W_1 in Figure 4. At this wage rate, entrepreneurs only wish to employ a labour force of E_1, but E_2 workers wish to supply their labour. The resulting unemployment (measured by E_2 minus E_1) is called **real wage unemployment** or **classical unemployment**.

If the price mechanism works efficiently in the labour market, the unemployment depicted in Figure 4 should only be temporary. W_1 is a **disequilibrium wage rate**. There is **excess supply of labour** (equal to the real wage unemployment) at this wage rate. As in any market, the market mechanism should come into play to eliminate the excess supply and restore equilibrium. To put it another way, some of the workers who want to work at the real wage rate W_1 (but who are unable to obtain employment at this wage) will offer their services at a lower wage rate. By undercutting the pay of those already in work, the wage rate will be bid down to W_{FE}, thereby restoring equilibrium (and full employment) in the labour market. But if wages are sticky, perhaps because labour markets are insufficiently competitive, real-wage unemployment may persist.

Even at full employment with the labour market clearing, there is always some unemployment. Change is constantly taking place in a dynamic economy, with some industries declining and others growing. As new products are developed and demand and cost conditions change, firms demand more of some labour skills while the demand for other types of labour declines. Economists use the term **frictional** and **structural unemployment** to describe the resulting unemployment.

Frictional unemployment, as its name suggests, results from frictions in the labour market which create a delay or time-lag during which a worker is unemployed when moving from one job to another. Note that our definition of frictional unemployment assumes that a job vacancy exists and that a friction in the job market, caused by either the **geographical or the occupational immobility of labour**, prevents an unemployed worker from filling the vacancy. It follows that the number of unfilled job vacancies which exist can be used as an indicator of the level of frictional unemployment in the economy. **Casual** and **seasonal unemployment** are special cases of frictional unemployment.

Structural unemployment is more severe, resulting from the **structural decline of industries** which are unable to compete or adapt in the face of changing demand and new products, new techniques of producing existing products and the emergence of more efficient competitors in other countries. The **growth of international competition** and the **globalisation** of the economy have contributed recently to structural unemployment. **Technological unemployment** can be regarded as a **special case of structural unemployment** which results from the successful growth of new industries using labour-saving technology such as **automation**.

Economists generally agree that **deficient aggregate demand** causes unemployment in recessions, though free-market economists regard demand-deficiency as less significant than Keynesian economists. **Demand-deficient unemployment** is also known as **cyclical** or **Keynesian** unemployment (after Keynes, who first identified demand-deficiency as an important possible cause of unemployment).

The appropriate policy to reduce unemployment depends on identifying correctly the underlying cause of unemployment. Expansionary monetary and/or fiscal policies are appropriate for reducing cyclical unemployment in recessions, but may fall foul of the **policy conflicts** described on pp. 20–21. The conflict between low unemployment and controlling inflation is particularly significant.

Inflation is defined as a persistent or continuing tendency for the price level to rise. Strictly, **deflation** is the opposite (a persistent tendency for the price level to fall), though economists usually use the word to refer to the reduction in output and employment which occur in recessions. When the government deflates the economy it uses contractionary monetary and/or fiscal policy to reduce the level of demand and economic activity. Conversely, the government **reflates** the economy when it uses monetary and/or fiscal policy to expand demand.

Too much or inappropriate expansion of demand leads to inflation of the price level rather than to reflation of output and employment. For example, if unemployment is incorrectly diagnosed in terms of demand deficiency (when the true cause is structural), a policy of fiscal or monetary expansion to stimulate aggregate demand creates **excess demand**. This in turn pulls up the price level with no lasting beneficial effects upon employment and creates a type of inflation which is called **demand-pull inflation**. The demand-pull theory of inflation is favoured by free-market and monetarist economists. In the **monetarist theory of demand-pull inflation**, the excess demand which pulls up the price level is blamed on an excess rate of growth of the **money supply**.

By contrast, many Keynesian economists favour the **cost-push** theory of inflation which argues that **monopoly power** is responsible for inflation. Trade unions bargain for money wage increases in excess of any rise in labour productivity. Monopoly firms are prepared to pay these wage increases because they can pass on the increasing costs as price rises. In the cost-push theory, trade union militancy and big business have been blamed for inflation.

Examination skills

The skills most likely to be tested by multiple-choice and data-response questions on employment, unemployment and inflation are as follows:

- Explaining employment in terms of the demand for, and supply of, labour.
- Relating the growth of employment to the growth of national income and output, and the resulting job creation.
- Defining and illustrating full employment in terms of a supply and demand diagram such as Figure 4.
- Explaining the main types of unemployment — frictional, structural etc.
- Understanding how unemployment is measured in the UK.
- Explaining the meaning of inflation and related terms such deflation and reflation.
- Analysing inflation in terms of the two main theories of inflation: demand-pull and cost-pull.
- Explaining and justifying appropriate policies to reduce unemployment and/or inflation.
- Understanding the policy conflict between low unemployment and low inflation.

Examination questions

You should expect up to three multiple-choice questions on the terms and concepts listed in specification section 11.1 on this topic. Of the questions included in the Question and Answer section of this guide, MCQs 6, 7 and 8 in Test 1 and 5 and 6 in Test 2 provide typical examples. DRQ 4 focuses on the policy conflict between low unemployment and low inflation, while DRQ 5 asks candidates to explain why economists have expected inflation to increase as unemployment falls and why this relationship did not hold in the late 1990s, 2000 and 2001.

Common examination errors

Commonly made mistakes on employment, unemployment and inflation include:
- Failure to provide an adequate definition of full employment.
- Rewriting a question so that you can write all you know about the different types of unemployment.
- Failure to relate policies to reduce unemployment to causes of unemployment.
- Confusing demand-pull and cost-push causes of inflation.
- Confusing inflation with one-off price rises and with changes in the relative prices of goods and services.
- Failure to understand data on inflation presented in index number form.

Aggregate demand

These notes relate to AQA specification section 11.2 and prepare you to answer AQA examination questions on:
- the nature and determinants of aggregate demand
- aggregate demand and the level of economic activity

Essential information

Aggregate demand comprises **total planned spending on goods and services** produced by the economy. (It measures **planned spending**, whereas the closely related concept of **national expenditure** measures *realised* or *actual* spending which has already taken place.) Four types of spending are included in aggregate demand, each type originating in a different **sector** of the economy: households, firms, the government sector and the overseas sector. The four sources of aggregate demand are shown in the following equation:

aggregate demand = consumption + investment + government spending + exports

(net of taxation)   (net of imports)

or:
$$AD = C + I + (G - T) + (X - M)$$

where C, I, G, T, X and M are consumption, investment, government spending, taxation, exports and imports.

The components of aggregate demand are illustrated in the circular flow diagram shown in Figure 5 where the dashed flow lines represent the **real flows** occurring in the economy between households and firms. Households supply labour and other factor services in exchange for goods and services produced by the firms. But the real flows generate **money flows** of income and expenditure shown by the solid flow lines.

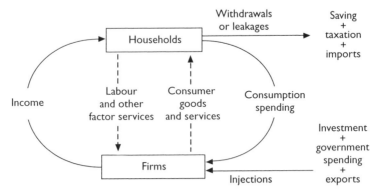

Figure 5 The components of aggregate demand and the circular flow of income

Figure 5 shows the incomes paid by firms to households, recirculating back to the firms when spent by the households on **consumption**. But households may save rather than spend part of their incomes. **Saving** — along with **taxation** and spending on **imports** — are **leakages** or **withdrawals** from the circular flow of income. By contrast, **investment**, **government spending** and spending by the rest of the world on the economy's **exports** are **injections** into the circular flow. Withdrawal from and injections into the circular flow are shown respectively by the horizontal arrows in Figure 5. If planned withdrawals of spending equal planned injections of spending into the flow, national income is in equilibrium and tends neither to rise nor fall. If withdrawals exceed injections, the resulting net leakage of spending from the circular flow causes output and income to fall. In this case, national income is in **disequilibrium**, and **deficient aggregate demand** would cause a **recession**.

This process shows that a decrease in aggregate demand induces further falls in spending and economic activity. Conversely, an increase in aggregate demand stimulates the economy and causes further increases in demand and output. Suppose, for example, that an increase in consumer confidence causes consumption to rise by £10 billion. This injection into the circular flow of income raises the incomes of shop keepers who benefit from increased consumer spending. Because their income has increased, people employed in the retail sector now spend more on consumption. The process continues in a ripple effect (known as the **multiplier**) spreading through the economy.

The components of aggregate demand have different determinants and this explains why injections may not equal withdrawals. **Income** is an important determinant of **consumption spending** by households. The higher a person's **disposable income**, the more he or she will wish to spend on consumer goods and services. However, the proportion of income consumed falls as income rises and the proportion saved increases. **Expected future income** also influences consumption and saving. At some stages in their lives, people spend more than their current incomes when, for example, they borrow to fund a house purchase in the hope that future income will enable them to repay the debt. Also, many people may save in mid-life to finance their retirement years. Consumption increases as **wealth** and **consumer confidence** increase. Houses and shares are important forms of wealth. Recessions can be caused when consumer spending falls following a sudden collapse in house or share prices.

Availability of credit provided by banks, and the cost of borrowing or credit (the **rate of interest**) are other determinants of consumption and saving. The rate of interest is also an important determinant of **investment** spending on capital goods by firms. For households, savings fall and consumption rises as rates of interest fall. Likewise, investment spending by firms increases as rates of interest fall. Investment projects deemed unprofitable at a higher cost of borrowing become profitable when cheaper finance is available. Other determinants of investment include **business confidence** and **technical progress**. A fast rate of technical progress means that existing capital equipment becomes obsolete or out of date and must be replaced. In 1999 and 2000, rapid technical progress in information and communication technology (ICT) created an investment boom in internet-based industries and mobile phone companies.

The government is a source of aggregate demand in the economy (**government spending**) and — through **taxation** — is also responsible for a major leakage of spending from the circular flow of income. The net effect of government on aggregate demand depends on the nature of the government's budget. There are three possibilities:
(1) A **budget deficit**, when government spending is greater than tax revenue, represents **expansionary fiscal policy** with the government injecting spending and demand into the economy.
(2) A **budget surplus** is the opposite. There is a net leakage of spending out of the economy as tax revenue exceeds government spending. Fiscal policy is contractionary.
(3) The government may **balance its budget** (setting G = T), which has a neutral effect on aggregate demand.

Planned spending on UK **exports** by residents of other countries increases aggregate demand, but planned spending on **imports** by UK residents reduces aggregate demand. The effect of the **overseas sector** on aggregate demand is rather similar to that of the government in that there are three possibilities:
(1) Balance of payments surplus: X > M. This injects spending into the economy and increases aggregate demand.
(2) Balance of payments deficit: X < M. This withdraws spending from the economy and is deflationary, reducing aggregate demand.
(3) Balance of payments equilibrium: X = M. This has a neutral effect on aggregate demand.

Examination skills

The skills most likely to be tested by multiple-choice and data-response questions on aggregate demand are as follows:

- Defining aggregate demand and identifying its components — consumption, investment etc.
- Explaining briefly the determinants of the main components of aggregate demand.
- Drawing and explaining briefly an aggregate demand curve (see next topic).
- Identifying and explaining the factors which cause an AD curve to shift.
- Explaining how an increase or decrease in aggregate demand may affect the economy.
- Explaining how fiscal and/or monetary policy may affect aggregate demand.
- Evaluating the effects of an increase or decrease in aggregate demand.

Examination questions

You should expect up to three multiple-choice questions on the terms and concepts listed in specification section 11.2 on this topic. Of the questions included in the Question and Answer section of this guide, MCQs 9 and 11 in Test 1 and 7, 8 and 9 in Test 2 provide typical examples. DRQ 2 focuses on how changes in consumption and investment may affect economic activity, while the scenario for DRQ 6 covers the relationship between the state of the economy and some of the components of aggregate demand.

Common examination errors

Commonly made mistakes on aggregate demand include the following:
- Confusing aggregate planned spending (aggregate demand) with national expenditure, which records spending that has already taken place in the economy.
- Confusing saving (the decision not to spend income) and investment (planned spending on capital goods).
- Inability to appreciate how fiscal and/or monetary policy may affect aggregate demand.
- Confusing withdrawals or leakages of demand from the circular flow of income with injections into the flow.
- Failure to relate the components of aggregate demand to the aggregate demand curve.
- Failure to appreciate that an initial increase in aggregate demand is likely to induce further increases in demand and economic activity.

The AD/AS macroeconomic model

These notes relate to AQA specification section 11.2 and prepare you to answer AQA examination questions on the:
- determinants of aggregate supply
- AD and AS curves
- use of AD/AS diagrams for analysing economic policy

Essential information

As its name suggests, an **aggregate demand/aggregate supply (AD/AS) diagram** contains an **aggregate demand (AD) curve** and an **aggregate supply (AS) curve**. The AD curves in Figure 6 are simply the sum of all the components of aggregate demand explained in the previous topic on p. 25.

The *slope* of each AD curve shows that aggregate demand for real output (goods and services) increases the lower the average price level in the economy. If any of the components of aggregate demand change, the AD curve *shifts* to a new position. For example, an increase in consumption, investment or export demand shifts the AD curve rightwards (from AD_1 to AD_2 in Figure 6), as would an expansionary fiscal or monetary policy.

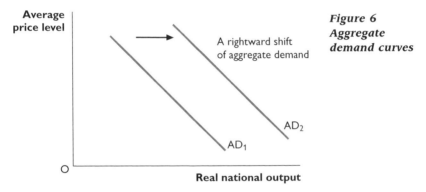

*Figure 6
Aggregate
demand curves*

Just as **aggregate demand** comprises the total spending upon national output which the economic agents in the economy wish or *plan* to undertake, so **aggregate supply** represents the total output of goods and services which the firms or producers in the economy wish or *plan* to supply and sell. Figure 7 illustrates two upward-sloping **short-run aggregate supply (SRAS) curves**.

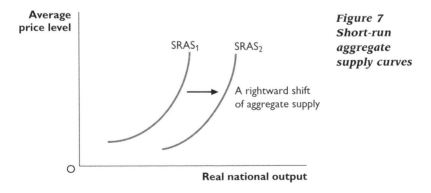

*Figure 7
Short-run
aggregate
supply curves*

The *short run* refers to the assumption that the economy's productive capacity is fixed (whereas capacity in the long run can be increased or decreased). The *position* of the SRAS curve in Figure 7 is determined by a number of factors, including costs of production, technology, attitudes, enterprise, factor mobility, the institutional structure of the economy, and the existence of economic incentives. If any of these change, the SRAS curve *shifts* to a new position. For example, a fall in production costs caused by lower labour costs or lower costs of imported raw materials or energy would shift the SRAS rightwards from $SRAS_1$ to $SRAS_2$ in Figure 7. The *slope* of the SRAS curve is derived from two assumptions:

(1) The cost of producing each extra unit of output rises in the short run.

(2) Because of rising costs, firms are only prepared to produce and supply more output if prices rise to enable the output to be sold profitably.

The three panels of Figure 8 show some of the ways in which the AD/AS macro-economic model can be used to explain and analyse the national economy.

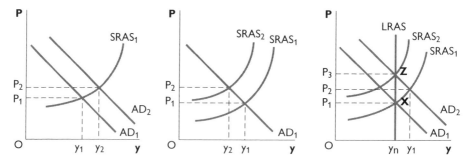

Figure 8 Using the AD/AS model to analyse the national economy

The left-hand panel illustrates the short-run effects of a rightward shift of aggregate demand along an upward-sloping SRAS curve. The increase in AD (caused, for example, by expansionary fiscal or monetary policy, or by an increase in consumption) *reflates* real national income or output from y_1 to y_2, and *inflates* the price level from P_1 to P_2. This diagram can be used to illustrate **demand-pull inflation**, since excess demand pulls up the price level.

By contrast, the middle panel of Figure 8 illustrates **cost-push inflation**. Increased production costs in the economy shift the short-run AS curve upwards or leftwards from $SRAS_1$ to $SRAS_2$. The price level is pushed up from P_1 to P_2 and, unless aggregate demand increases, national output falls from y_1 to y_2. Conversely, if production costs fall, then the SRAS curve shifts rightwards, causing the price level to fall and output to increase.

As previously noted, the aggregate supply curves in the left-hand and middle panels of Figure 8 are *short-run* AS curves, drawn under the assumption that the economy's productive capacity is fixed. By contrast, the right-hand panel includes a vertical **long-run aggregate supply (LRAS) curve**. Supply-side economists use the vertical LRAS curve to argue that in the long-run expansionary fiscal and monetary policies cannot increase real national income or output beyond y_n. This is called the **natural level of output** by free-market economists. Point X in the right-hand panel of Figure 8 shows the economy in an initial state of **macroeconomic equilibrium**, where AD_1

equals both $SRAS_1$ and LRAS. If the government increases aggregate demand from AD_1 to AD_2, output temporarily rises above its natural level to y_1 and the price level also rises to P_2.

However, according to free-market economists, output cannot be sustained above its natural level. Increased costs of production shift the short-run AS curve leftwards to $SRAS_2$ and a new macroeconomic equilibrium at point Z. At the new macroeconomic equilibrium, national output has fallen back to its natural level y_n, but at the cost of a significantly higher price level P_3. Free-market and supply-side economists argue that it is irresponsible for governments to expand demand to increase output and employment above their natural levels. In their view, the only long-term effect is to cause inflation.

Examination skills

The skills most likely to be tested by multiple-choice and data-response questions on the AD/AS macroeconomic model are as follows:
- Distinguishing between the factors determining aggregate demand and aggregate supply.
- Interpreting AD/AS diagrams in multiple-choice questions.
- Using AD/AS diagrams in a relevant way to analyse events described in a data-response question.
- Explaining that the effects resulting from an increase in aggregate demand depend on the shape of the AS curve.
- Distinguishing between short-run and long-run aggregate supply (SRAS and LRAS).
- Illustrating demand-pull and/or cost-push inflation using AD/AS diagrams.
- Illustrating expansionary fiscal policy and/or monetary policy using AD/AS diagrams.

Examination questions

You should expect up to three multiple-choice questions on the terms and concepts listed in specification section 11.2 on this topic. Of the questions included in the Question and Answer section of this guide, MCQs 8, 12, 13 and 14 in Test 1 and 9 in Test 2 provide typical examples. The AD/AS macroeconomic model is unlikely to figure explicitly in a data-response question, but many DRQs can be answered by applying the model to analyse the problems affecting the UK economy and the impact of government policy. Part (c) of DRQs 3, 4 and 5 provide examples.

Common examination errors

Commonly made mistakes on the AD/AS macroeconomic model include the following:
- Confusing AD and AS curves.
- Confusing short-run and long-run aggregate supply curves (SRAS and LRAS).
- Mislabelling the axes of AD/AS diagrams (e.g. writing 'inflation' instead of 'the price level' on the vertical axis, or 'employment' rather than 'national output' or 'real output' on the horizontal axis).

- Failure to identify the factors that can cause the AD curve and/or the AS curve to shift.
- Confusing macroeconomic AD/AS diagrams with microeconomic supply and demand diagrams.

Fiscal policy

These notes relate to AQA specification section 11.3 and prepare you to answer AQA examination questions on:
- the meaning of fiscal policy
- how fiscal policy can influence the economy
- important tax and public spending concepts

Essential information

Fiscal policy is the part of a government's economic policy aimed at achieving its economic **objectives** through the use of the **fiscal instruments** of **taxation**, **public spending** and the **budget deficit** or **surplus**. For many years, fiscal policy was generally associated with **managing the level of aggregate demand** in order to expand (reflate) or contract (deflate) the economy. This was known as **Keynesian** fiscal policy. To increase aggregate demand, the government increased government spending and/or cut taxes. The resulting increase in the government's budget deficit injected demand into the circular flow of income. Contractionary fiscal policy involved the opposite: cuts in government spending and/or tax increases which reduced the budget deficit, possibly moving the government's finances into surplus. It took demand out of the economy and was also called **discretionary fiscal policy**. Tax rates and levels of public spending were **fine-tuned** or regularly adjusted to try to maintain a high level of employment while avoiding an unacceptable increase in the rate of inflation.

The fiscal policy pursued in recent years in the UK has been different from the Keynesian one described above. For the most part, fiscal policy has been used as part of a wider supply-side policy to increase the role of markets and the private sector's economic activity and to reduce the economic role of the state. Under monetarist and supply-side influence, recent UK governments have believed that a policy of stimulating or reflating aggregate demand to achieve growth and full employment is, in the long run, at best ineffective and at worst damaging. Monetarists have argued that any growth of output and employment resulting from an expansionary fiscal policy is short-lived. They say the main effect of such a policy is the **inflation** which quickly destroys the conditions necessary for satisfactory market performance and wealth creation. Fiscal policy is now used to **create stability** in the economy, and economic agents, particularly businesses, are not subjected to **sudden surprises** in the form of unexpected tax changes. The government now often announces proposed changes to taxation and public spending in its **autumn review** several months before they are formally introduced in the following **March budget**.

The **microeconomic elements of fiscal policy** have also become significant, with an emphasis on **fiscal incentives** aimed at improving economic performance on the supply side. It is argued that **lower rates of income tax** increase incentives to **save**, **work harder** and be **entrepreneurial**. On the public spending side of fiscal policy, changes to the benefits system (particularly **unemployment benefits**) have been made to alter the labour/leisure choice in favour of working rather than choosing voluntary unemployment. DRQ 4 on p. 75 provides details of current UK fiscal policy.

To some extent, fiscal policy is now subordinated to the needs of monetary policy. Monetarists believe that excessive levels of public spending and public borrowing contribute to excessive monetary growth and hence to inflation. UK governments now try to restrict public spending and borrowing to levels and rates of growth deemed consistent with achieving control over monetary growth and inflation.

Some fiscal policy terms and concepts that are useful to know are outlined below.

Public sector's net cash requirement (PSNCR)

Whenever the government spends more on its public spending programme than it raises in taxes and from other sources of revenue, borrowing must finance the resulting budget deficit. Until recently, this flow of borrowing was called the **public sector borrowing requirement (PSBR)**, though it is now known as the PSNCR. By contrast, when revenues exceed expenditure and there is a budget surplus, the surplus tax revenue can be used to repay previous government borrowing or debt. This is called the **public sector debt repayment (PSDR)**.

The national debt

Whereas the budget deficit, the PSNCR and related concepts are all examples of economic *flows*, the national debt is a *stock*. It is the accumulation of central government debt that has built up over time. Whenever there is a budget deficit, the *flow* of new borrowing adds to the *stock* of debt. Conversely, repayment of debt in the event of a budget surplus reduces the national debt.

Types of taxation and government spending

The two main types of taxes are **income taxes** and **taxes on expenditure** such as value added tax (VAT). In recent years, fiscal policy has generally altered the **structure of taxation** away from income taxes to taxes on spending, in the belief that expenditure taxes have fewer harmful effects on supply-side incentives than income tax. However, as the petrol price rebellion of autumn 2000 showed, there may be a limit to the extent to which the government can raise expenditure taxes without facing a taxpayers' revolt. Income taxes are **direct taxes**, whereas most expenditure taxes are **indirect taxes**. Taxation is **progressive** or **regressive**. UK income tax is progressive as a larger proportion of income is paid in tax as income rises. Conversely, expenditure taxes, such as the duty on tobacco, tend to be regressive — a smaller proportion of income is paid in tax as income rises. The main purpose of taxation is to raise revenue to finance government spending. Government spending can be divided into:

(1) The **direct production and provision of goods and services**, e.g. **public goods**, such as police and roads, and **merit goods**, such as health care and education.

(2) Payment of **transfer incomes** such as welfare benefits, e.g. the state pension and unemployment benefits.

(3) Interest payments on the national debt.

The government spending multiplier

This measures the relationship between an increase in government spending and the resulting change in national income. For example, a government spending multiplier of 5 means that an increase of £1 billion in government spending causes national income to increase by £5 billion. The bigger the multiplier, the more powerful is fiscal policy when used to influence the economy through management of aggregate demand. However, because a substantial fraction of an increase in aggregate demand leaks into taxation and imports, the multiplier is probably not very large. You should also note that an increase in aggregate demand may *inflate* the price level rather than *reflate* real output, especially when the economy approaches full employment.

Examination skills

The skills most likely to be tested by multiple-choice and data-response questions on fiscal policy are as follows:

- Defining fiscal policy and distinguishing it from monetary policy.
- Understanding the link between fiscal policy and monetary policy, e.g. via the government's borrowing requirement.
- Explaining how fiscal policy can be used to manage aggregate demand and discussing the limitations of using fiscal policy in this way.
- Illustrating demand-side fiscal policy on an AD/AS diagram and explaining how the effectiveness of the policy depends on the nature of aggregate supply.
- Describing and explaining the main elements of the more supply-side fiscal policy implemented in the UK in recent years.
- Relating fiscal policy to the macroeconomic policy objectives of full employment, growth and controlling inflation.
- Applying in a relevant way fiscal policy concepts such as the budget deficit or surplus, the borrowing requirement or net cash requirement etc.

Examination questions

You should expect up to three multiple-choice questions on the terms and concepts listed in specification section 11.3 on this topic, though only one or two may focus exclusively on fiscal policy. Of the questions included in the Question and Answer section of this guide, MCQs 7, 11 and 12 in Test 1 and 5, 6, 10 and 12 in Test 2 make some mention of fiscal policy, taxation or government spending, but only MCQ 10 in Test 2 solely relates to fiscal policy. DRQ 3 tests knowledge and understanding of the nature of UK fiscal policy and this knowledge is also relevant for answering part (c) of DRQs 2 and 4.

Common examination errors

Commonly made mistakes on fiscal policy include the following:

- Confusing fiscal policy with monetary policy.
- Wrongly asserting that fiscal policy is currently used to manage aggregate demand.
- Inability to use an AD/AS diagram to illustrate the impact of fiscal policy on the national economy.
- Confusing a budget deficit (or surplus) with a balance of payments deficit (or surplus).
- Inability to relate a budget deficit (or surplus) to injections into (or withdrawals from) the circular flow of income.
- Failure to understand that many aspects of recent and current fiscal policy in the UK illustrate supply-side economic policy.
- Poor understanding of terms such as 'progressive and regressive taxation' and 'direct and indirect taxation'.

Monetary policy

These notes relate to AQA specification section 11.3 and prepare you to answer AQA examination questions on the:

- meaning of monetary policy
- main features of UK monetary policy
- impact of monetary policy on the national economy

Essential information

Monetary policy can be defined as any deliberate action undertaken by the government or its agents, such as the country's **central bank**, to achieve economic objectives through the use of monetary instruments like **controls over bank lending** and the **rate of interest**. Until 1997, UK monetary policy was implemented more or less jointly by the **Treasury** (the government's finance ministry) and the **Bank of England**. The two institutions were known as the **monetary authorities**. In 1997, the Bank of England was made independent and it is now the sole monetary authority, with a duty to implement monetary policy to achieve the monetary policy target set by the Treasury.

While there are a number of **monetary policy instruments** (such as controls over bank lending) which could be used, recent and current monetary policy has used a single policy instrument, **interest rates**, to try to achieve a single objective, namely **control of inflation**. Under the influence of free-market, supply-side and monetarist theory, more interventionist monetary policy instruments have been abandoned on the grounds that they create inefficiencies and make the banking system uncompetitive.

To understand monetary policy, it is useful to distinguish between its **ultimate** and **intermediate** objectives. For over 20 years, **control of inflation** has been the *ultimate* objective of monetary policy. However, the *intermediate* objectives of monetary policy have changed during these years. The three phases of monetary policy have been:

(1) The money supply as the intermediate objective of monetary policy. In the early 1980s, monetary policy aimed to achieve price stability by first controlling the rate of growth of money supply. The authorities used monetary policy to try to hit a published **money supply target** which functioned as an intermediate policy objective. This policy was abandoned, largely because, as soon as policy tried to control growth of the money supply, the linkage between the money supply and inflation broke down.

(2) The exchange rate as the intermediate objective of monetary policy. Between the mid-1980s and 1992, the **exchange rate** replaced the money supply as the inter-mediate target of monetary policy. Interest rates were raised to support a high exchange rate (which from 1990 to 1992 was fixed within the **exchange rate mechanism (ERM)** of the **European monetary system (EMS)**). A high exchange rate can help to reduce inflation in two ways. First, it reduces inflation directly by lowering prices of imported food, energy, raw materials and consumer goods. Second (and less directly), high exchange rates mean UK firms are likely to lose markets if they raise prices more than their overseas competitors do. This pressurises firms into reducing inflationary price increases, whilst fear of job losses pressurises workers to settle for lower pay increases.

(3) Targeting the inflation rate directly. Intermediate targets of monetary policy were dropped in 1992 when the pound was withdrawn from the ERM fixed exchange rate system. Monetary policy is now directed explicitly at a **published inflation rate target**.

The main features of current UK monetary policy are:

(1) Monetary policy is implemented by the Bank of England's **Monetary Policy Committee (MPC)** to achieve an inflation target set by the government, which was initially 2.5%.

(2) The policy instrument used to achieve this is a change in the **Bank of England's official interest rate**. This is the rate of interest at which the Bank of England lends to the UK banking system. A change in the Bank of England's interest rate quickly affects other short-term interest rates (such as the overdraft rates banks charge to personal and business customers), and usually affects mortgage interest rates at which homeowners borrow long term.

(3) Although dropped as intermediate policy targets, information about the money supply and the exchange rate are used (along with a number of other key statistics) as indicators of whether the policy is on course.

(4) Monetary policy is **pre-emptive**. Policy-makers at the Bank of England estimate what the inflation rate is likely to be 18 months to 2 years ahead (the medium term) if policy (i.e. interest rates) remains unchanged. If the forecast rate of inflation is too far away from the target rate set by the government, the Bank will change interest rates immediately to prevent the forecast inflation rate becoming a reality. The Bank is also prepared to raise or lower interest rates to pre-empt or head-off any likely adverse effects upon the inflation rate of an outside shock affecting the economy.

Transparency and accountability are central and the MPC's performance in implementing monetary policy is subject to Parliamentary scrutiny. The target for inflation applies at all times and the MPC is accountable for any deviations from it. If inflation is more than 1% higher or lower than the target, the open letter system requires that the governor of the Bank of England writes to the chancellor explaining why the divergence has occurred. Any such letter must be published to facilitate public scrutiny.

Significantly, the inflation rate target is now symmetrical. Prior to May 1997, monetary policy was concerned only with getting the inflation rate at or *below* the target 2.5% rate. Critics argued that the policy had a built-in deflationary bias. This is no longer the case, because the MPC is prepared to reduce interest rates to stimulate output and employment if it believes that on unchanged policies, an inflation rate below 2.5% will be accompanied by an undesirable fall in output and employment. In the government's words: 'The primary objective of monetary policy is price stability. But subject to that, the Bank of England must also support the government's economic policy objectives, including those for growth and employment.'

Some commentators argue that monetary policy is being used in a Keynesian way to manage aggregate demand. However, current policy differs in significant ways from the Keynesian demand management policies practised for many years. First, only monetary policy, and not fiscal policy, is used to manage demand (the fiscal policy framework explained in the previous topic on pp. 32–35 is most definitely non-discretionary). Second, control of inflation rather than full employment remains the principal (but not the only) policy objective. Third, control of inflation is regarded as a pre-condition for the success of the government's supply-side policies. Fourth, monetary policy is implemented by an independent Bank of England, which is unlikely — unless leaned on by the government — to succumb to the temptation to engineer an inflationary boom.

Examination skills

The skills most likely to be tested by multiple-choice and data-response questions on monetary policy are as follows:
- Defining monetary policy and distinguishing it from fiscal policy.
- Relating monetary policy to the objectives of macroeconomic policy, particularly the control of inflation.
- Interpreting performance indicators such as the RPI data, index of average earnings, money supply, interest rate and exchange rate data.
- Explaining how monetary policy affects aggregate demand.
- Illustrating the effects of monetary policy on an AD/AS diagram and explaining the main elements of the more supply-side fiscal policy implemented in the UK in recent years.

Examination questions

You should expect up to three multiple-choice questions on the terms and concepts listed in specification section 11.3 on this topic, though only one or two may focus exclusively on monetary policy. Of the questions included in the Question and Answer section of this guide, MCQs 7 and 9 in Test 1 and 3 and 4 in Test 2 make some mention of monetary policy. DRQ 3 tests knowledge and understanding of the nature of UK monetary policy and this knowledge is also relevant for answering part (c) of DRQs 2 and 4.

Common examination errors

Commonly made mistakes on monetary policy include the following:
- Confusing monetary policy with both fiscal policy and supply-side policy.
- Treating monetarism and monetary policy as interchangeable terms.
- Confusing the instruments and objectives of monetary policy.
- Inability to use an AD/AS diagram to illustrate the impact of monetary policy on the national economy.
- Failure to understand how monetary policy affects the exchange rate, and how the exchange rate affects monetary policy.
- Failure to appreciate that the rate of interest is the key instrument in monetary policy.
- Confusing the roles of the government and the Bank of England respectively in setting the objectives and implementing monetary policy.

Supply-side policies

These notes relate to AQA specification section 11.3 and prepare you to answer AQA examination questions on the:
- meaning of supply-side policies
- main features of UK supply-side policy
- impact of supply-side policy on the national economy

Essential information

Before the 1980s, macroeconomic policy generally meant demand management. However, in the 1980s and 1990s, economic policy switched away from the *demand side* to the *supply side* of the economy. Economists now generally agree that, except in recessions, the major problems facing the UK economy are the supply-side problems of producing goods and services that are both quality-competitive and price-competitive in domestic and export markets.

Supply-side policies are a response to increasingly fierce international competition and they aim to change the underlying structure of the economy and improve all-round economic performance. Many supply-side policies are *microeconomic* rather than *macroeconomic*, since they act on the motivation and efficiency of individual economic agents in order to improve general economic performance and underlying production potential. If successful, such policies also have a macroeconomic effect through **shifting the economy's long-run aggregate supply curve rightwards**.

Supply-side microeconomic policy is pro-market and anti-interventionist. It attempts to change the economic function of government from **provider** to **enabler**. Supply-side policies aim to **promote entrepreneurship** and **popular capitalism**, replacing the **dependency culture** and **statism** which — for the supply-siders — are the legacy of previous demand-side economic policy.

Supply-side economists argue that when fiscal policy is used to manage demand, the average tax rate may increase beyond a critical point at which tax revenue is maximised. Any further tax increases have the perverse effect of reducing the government's total tax revenue. Indeed, supply-side economists recommend tax cuts to stimulate the economy, believing that this will generate more tax revenue at lower rates of tax.

Figure 9 shows how supply-side economists contrast the macroeconomic effects of demand-side and supply-side policies. They believe that the AS curve is vertical (in the long run), and that the vertical AS curve is located at the economy's natural or equilibrium level of real output, which is the level of output consistent with the natural rate of unemployment in the labour market. The left-hand panel illustrates the supply-side view that the main effect of an expansion of aggregate demand is inflation.

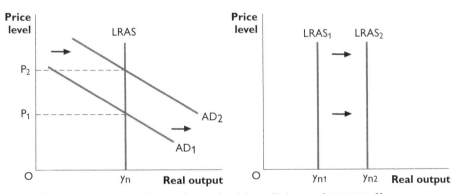

Figure 9 Demand-side and supply-side policies and AD/AS diagrams

If we assume that the economy is initially at its natural or equilibrium level of output y_n, an increase in aggregate demand from AD_1 to AD_2 triggers demand inflation which pulls the price level up from P_1 to P_2. By contrast, supply-side policies shift the LRAS curve rightwards (from $LRAS_1$ to $LRAS_2$ in the right-hand panel of Figure 9), thereby increasing the natural levels of output and employment. In the supply-side view, demand management policies should be restricted to stimulating the economy (via interest rate cuts) when the economy is in recession (and output is *below* its natural level) and to reducing aggregate demand (by increasing interest rates) when there is a danger of demand-pull inflation. Fiscal policy should be used as part of supply-side policy, and *not* to manage demand.

Supply-side policies can be grouped into three main categories:
(1) Industrial policy measures. These include: **privatisation** (the sale or transfer of assets such as nationalised industries from the **public sector** to the **private sector**);

marketisation (shifting economic activity from **non-market provision** financed by taxation to **market provision**); and **deregulation** (the removal of previously imposed regulations in order to promote competition by **removing barriers to market entry** and to **get rid of unnecessary red tape and bureaucracy** which raise firms' costs).

(2) Labour market measures. These include: **income tax cuts** to create labour market incentives; **reducing state welfare benefits** to create an incentive to choose low-paid employment rather than unemployment; **increasing labour market flexibility** by **reducing the powers of trade unions** and replacing **jobs for life** with **short-term labour contracts**; and **improving the training of labour**.

(3) Financial and capital market measures. These include: **deregulating financial markets** to create greater competition and lower borrowing costs; **encouraging saving** by granting **special tax privileges** for savings and the use of the **sale of shares in privatised industries** to encourage **wider share ownership; promoting entrepreneurship** via tax cuts; and **reduced public spending, budget deficits and government borrowing** to **free resources for private sector use**.

Examination skills

The skills most likely to be tested by multiple-choice and data-response questions on supply-side policies are as follows:

- Defining supply-side policies and distinguishing them from other instruments of economic policy.
- Identifying a range of supply-side policies.
- Relating supply-side policy to free-market views of how the economy works and the appropriate approach of economic policy to problems posed by the economy.
- Illustrating the impact of supply-side policies on an AD/AS diagram.
- Comparing and contrasting the effects of supply-side and demand-side policies.
- Evaluating the effectiveness of supply-side policy, perhaps with the aid of appropriate indicators of national economic performance such as productivity figures.

Examination questions

You should expect up to three multiple-choice questions on the terms and concepts listed in specification section 11.3 on this topic. Of the questions included in the Question and Answer section of this guide, MCQs 6 in Test 1 and 4 and 11 in Test 2 provide typical examples. Supply-side policies are relevant for discussion and evaluation of the issues posed in part (c) of DRQs 1, 3, 4 and 5.

Common examination errors

Commonly made mistakes on supply-side policies include the following:

- Confusing supply-side and demand-side policies.
- Confusing supply-side policies with controlling the money supply (which is monetary policy).
- Failing to realise that some, but not all, fiscal policies are examples of supply-side policies.

- Inaccurate drawing of AD/AS diagrams to illustrate the impact of supply-side policies.
- Confusing interventionist supply-side policies such as nationalisation with anti-interventionist supply-side policies such as privatisation.
- Failure to analyse and evaluate the effects of supply-side policies properly.

National economic performance

These notes relate in particular to AQA specification section 11.1 and more generally to the whole specification, and prepare you to answer AQA examination questions which require an understanding of the:
- performance of the UK economy in the recent past
- likely performance in future years
- indicators of national economic performance

Essential information

Data-response questions are likely to reflect the state of the UK economy up to 2 years before the date of the examination, though information from earlier years may also be included. To answer questions well, you must possess knowledge of the perform-ance of the UK economy over the 10 or so years before the examination. You must also be aware of the state of the economy at the time of the examination and the possible state of the economy up to 3 or 4 years ahead. Such knowledge is especially useful when the data in the question includes a projection or forecast for future years, e.g. future levels of output and employment. Also, part (c) of a DRQ might ask you to discuss the implications of the data for future economic policy or economic activity.

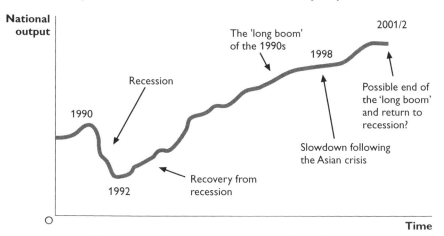

Figure 10 The UK's recent economic performance

Figure 10 summarises how UK national output changed in the 1990s and the early 2000s. It shows the:

- boom conditions of the late 1980s coming to an end in 1990
- severe **recession** from 1990 to 1992
- continued **economic growth** through most of the rest of the 1990s
- slowdown in 1998, partly caused by crisis and recession in southeast Asia
- renewed growth followed by slowdown again in 2001 and the possibility of a return to recession after 2002

Figure 10 illustrates the **business cycle**, which is also depicted in Figure 11, together with the economy's **trend rate of growth**. Until recently, the UK's trend rate of growth (or **long-term growth rate**) was about 2.2% a year. Actual growth was, of course, faster in the upswing of the business cycle (the **recovery** and **boom** phases) and negative in the recessionary phase. (A **recession** occurs when real national output falls for 6 months or more.) By the late 1990s, some economists believed that major **structural change** was taking place in the US economy, and perhaps also in the UK and other economies. They argued that structural change, partly caused by the impact of **information and communication technology (ICT)** upon the economy, had increased both labour productivity and the economy's trend rate of growth. The term 'New **Economy**' was coined. Optimists went further, arguing that future growth would not only be faster, but that business cycles would be milder and the threat of recession much reduced. However, the period of extreme optimism was short-lived. Share prices crashed in 2000 and 2001 (especially those of New Economy dot.com companies), aggregate demand fell, particularly in the US, and the threat of recession loomed once again. Following the adverse 'outside shock' caused by the terrorist attack on September 11th, 2001, few economists now argue that recessions are a thing of the past.

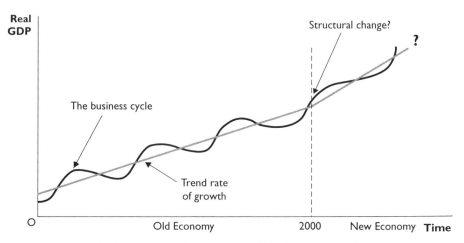

Figure 11 The business cycle and a possible increase in the economy's trend rate of growth

Nevertheless, recent UK governments succeeded (at least until 2002) in managing aggregate demand so as to control the business cycle and achieve sustained economic growth and falling unemployment, without accelerating inflation. Various factors contributed to this success, including:

- The effect of **supply-side policies**, which modernised the economy and made it more competitive.
- The generally **favourable state of the world economy**, including **falling commodity and oil prices**, until 1999.
- Competing in an increasingly **globalised economy**, which means UK firms and workers know that inflationary price and wage rises will be punished by loss of markets and jobs.
- The **success of monetary policy** in controlling inflation, particularly after the Bank of England was granted operational independence in 1997.

Another factor contributing to the success of UK macroeconomic policy — particularly monetary policy — has been the generally improved quality of information about the economy available to policy-makers. The **Office for National Statistics (ONS)** provides up-to-date information on a range of macroeconomic variables, including output, economic growth, employment, unemployment, wages, prices, the inflation rate and trade figures. These and other **performance indicators** are used to compare the performance of the UK economy with that of competitor countries. Whereas performance indicators monitor *current* and *recent* economic performance, **policy indicators** enable the government and Bank of England to assess whether current policy is on course to achieve desired targets.

Some economic variables are known as **lead variables** because they provide information about the future state of the economy (assuming unchanged government policy). **Surveys of consumer and business confidence** and **investment intentions** indicate the existence of a **feel-good** or **feel-bad factor** and provide information about the likely state of aggregate demand a few months ahead. Statistics for house-building starts and the number of people who have booked expensive summer or skiing holidays several months in advance also provide information about future spending, while data on commodity and input prices can signal future changes in retail price inflation. By contrast, employment and unemployment figures are better thought of as **lag variables** as they tend to *follow* rather than *lead* future economic activity.

Examination skills

The skills most likely to be tested by multiple-choice and data-response questions on national economic performance are as follows:

- Interpreting and analysing economic data covering a number of years to detect trends in the data.
- Separating cyclical and sometimes seasonal variations from the underlying trend.
- Calculating percentage growth rates, inflation rates, rates of increase of wages etc.
- Detecting correlations, which may sometimes be lagged, between variables such as employment and inflation.

- Appreciating the existence of leads and lags in economic data and whether a particular variable is best interpreted to indicate future or past economic performance.
- Understanding the contribution of a particular economic variable, e.g. productivity to national economic performance.

Examination questions

Some multiple-choice questions may include statistics relating to the performance of the national economy in the 10 years before the examination. You should expect up to five MCQs based on real-world data. Examples of statistics-based MCQs are MCQs 10 and 13 in Test 1 and 1, 14 and 15 in Test 2. Virtually every data-response question will contain data on the recent performance of the UK economy. Likewise, the DRQs will ask you to describe, explain and evaluate aspects of national economic perform-ance, and to assess the implications of the data for future economic performance. The six DRQs included in the next section of this guide illustrate what to expect.

Common examination errors

Commonly made mistakes on national economic performance include the following:
- A lack of knowledge and understanding of the performance of the UK economy over the 10 years before the examination.
- Inability to compare and interpret data relating to the UK economy and similar economies.
- Inability to detect important features of data such as the business cycle.
- Failure to apply general economic knowledge to help interpret data about national economic performance.
- A tendency to assume the future will always be a continuation of the present.
- The use of words such as 'vast' and 'massive' to describe quite small changes in national economic performance.
- Confusing data about national economic performance presented in index number form with percentage data.
- Failure to see the connections between different indicators of national economic performance.

Questions
&
Answers

This section includes 36 examination-style questions designed to be a key learning, revision and exam preparation resource. There are 30 multiple-choice questions (MCQs) and six data-response questions (DRQs). The 30 MCQs, which are set out in two 15-question tests (Test 1 and Test 2), are similar in layout, structure and style to complete ECN2/1 papers in the examination. The questions can be used *en bloc* as part of a trial or mock exam near the end of your course. Alternatively, as you study a topic in the Content Guidance section of this guide, you could refer selectively to particular MCQs in this section that assess aspects of the topic.

Likewise, you can use the DRQs as timed test questions in the lead-up to the examination, or topic by topic to reinforce your understanding as you proceed through Content Guidance.

This section also includes:
- Correct answers for the MCQs.
- Examiner's comments on the MCQs, explaining particular features of each question, or possible causes of difficulty.
- A student's answer of Grade A to C standard for each DRQ.
- Examiner's comments on each student's answer, explaining — where relevant — how the answer could be improved and a higher grade or mark achieved. These comments are denoted by the icon 🔁.

Note: It is important to understand the difference between two types of marks that the GCE examining boards award for candidates' work — 'raw marks' and uniform standardised marks (USMs).

Raw marks are the marks out of 25 awarded by the examiner who reads your script. After all the scripts have been marked, and basing their decisions only on raw marks, a grade-awarding panel decides where the grade boundaries should be set for each of the AS pass grades: A, B, C, D and E.

After all the grade boundaries have been set as raw marks, each candidate's raw mark for the Unit 2 paper is converted into a USM. Uniform standardised marks have the same grade boundaries — for all subjects and all unit exams. These are: grade A: 80%; grade B: 70%; grade C: 60%; grade D: 50%; grade E: 40%.

The marks awarded for candidates' answers for each of the DRQs in the following pages are raw marks and not USMs. A likely grade is indicated at the end of each candidate's answer, based on the qualities shown in each of the answer's three parts. It must be stressed that the actual raw mark at which a particular grade boundary is set varies from examination to examination, depending on factors such as whether the questions turned out to be relatively easy or relatively difficult, when compared to questions in previous examinations.

Multiple-choice questions: Test 1

1 The money national income for a country in 2003 is equal to:
- **A** The physical quantity of goods and services produced in the country in 2003
- **B** Real national income in 2003 adjusted for inflation
- **C** The monetary value of the stock of capital and consumer goods in the country at the end of 2003
- **D** Real national income produced by the country's economy during 2003 valued at 2003's prices

2 The diagram illustrates two production possibility frontiers for an economy, PP_1 and PP_2.

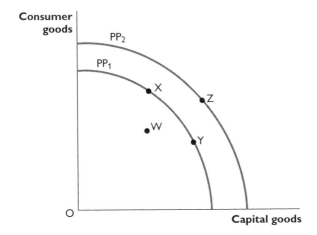

Which of the following statements relating to the diagram is NOT correct?
- **A** Economic growth is best defined as a movement from a point such as W to a point such as X or Y
- **B** If the economy is on the frontier PP_2, point Z but not point X or Y represents full employment
- **C** The movement from PP_1 to PP_2 shows economic growth taking place
- **D** If the economy is on the frontier PP_1, point Y is likely to produce a faster rate of growth than point X

3 Which one of the following would best indicate that inflation is taking place? A continuing increase in:
- **A** The value of money
- **B** Money national income
- **C** Relative prices
- **D** The price level

multiple-choice questions

4 Which of the following statements about macroeconomic policy objectives is correct?
   A UK governments always regard control of inflation as the most important policy objective
   B Because of conflicting objectives, macroeconomic policy is never successful
   C Expanding demand to reduce unemployment may worsen the balance of payments
   D The pursuit of economic growth inevitably increases inflation

5 An economy is experiencing the following problems simultaneously: a balance of payments deficit, accelerating inflation, high unemployment, and a growing inequality in the distribution of income. A decision by the government to reduce the standard rate of income tax by 5% and the higher rate by 20% would indicate that the macroeconomic objective of the tax cuts is to decrease the:
   A Balance of payments deficit
   B Inflation rate
   C Level of unemployment
   D Inequality in the distribution of income

6 A supply-side economist would recommend that in the long term, the UK unemployment problem should be tackled by:
   A A reduction in the money supply
   B Income tax cuts to promote labour market incentives
   C Tax cuts to expand aggregate demand
   D Increasing the Jobseekers' Allowance and the period for which it can be claimed

7 When the economy is in recession, which of the following is LEAST likely to reduce unemployment?
   A An expansionary fiscal policy
   B The Bank of England cutting interest rates
   C Retraining schemes for redundant workers
   D A new regulation extending employment rights for newly-hired workers

8 On an aggregate demand and aggregate supply diagram, cost-push inflation is shown by:
   A A leftward shift of the short-run aggregate supply curve
   B A rightward shift of the aggregate demand curve
   C A rightward shift of the long-run aggregate supply curve
   D A leftward shift of the aggregate demand curve

9 A fall in the rate of interest is likely to cause all the following EXCEPT:
   A Increased consumption
   B Increased investment
   C A higher exchange rate
   D An increase in aggregate demand

questions & answers

10 The chart below refers to UK gross domestic product (GDP), at 1995 prices, from 1990 to 2000.

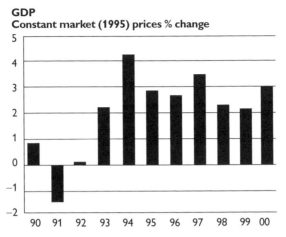

GDP
Constant market (1995) prices % change

Source: HM Treasury (in *The Guardian*, 4 April 2001).

The data show:

A Prices remaining at their 1995 levels from 1996 to 2000

B Real GDP falling after 1994

C Output of goods and services increasing for most of the period covered by the data

D Nominal GDP falling in 1991

11 A government with a budget deficit increases its spending but leaves taxation unchanged. Which of the following statements is NOT true?

A The government's borrowing requirement will increase

B The aggregate demand curve will shift to the right

C The initial change in government spending may lead to a larger impact upon the economy

D An expansionary monetary policy is being implemented

12 The diagram illustrates two aggregate supply curves for an economy.

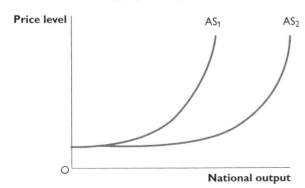

ultiple-choice questions

Which of the following events might cause the aggregate supply curve to shift from AS₁ to AS₂?

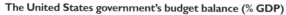

A An increase in the wages firms pay to workers

B An increase in the government's budget deficit

C Technical progress reducing firms' costs of production

D The price level rising, enabling firms to sell their output at higher prices

13

The United States government's budget balance (% GDP)

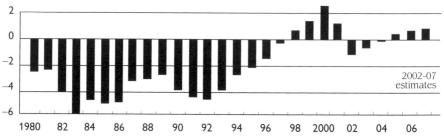

2002-07 estimates

From the data it can be concluded that:

A The United States balance of payments had a current account deficit for most of the period shown by the data

B The United States government's finances were in surplus in 2000 and 2001

C The United States government's national debt diminished in size from 1992 to 1997

D The United States economy was in recession in 2000 and 2001

14 The diagram depicts the aggregate demand and supply curves for an economy. The economy is initially in macroeconomic equilibrium at point X, with national output at y_1 and the price level at P_1.

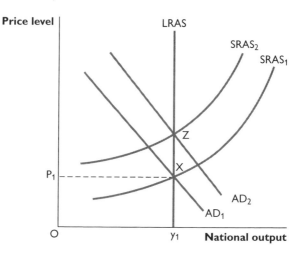

If the government expands demand, which of the following statements relating to the diagram is NOT correct?

A The aggregate demand curve will shift to AD_2, and then the short-run aggregate supply curve will shift to $SRAS_2$

B Macroeconomic equilibrium will be disturbed but eventually a new equilibrium occurs at point Z

C National output may increase temporarily above y_1

D Both national output and average prices will quickly return to their original levels y_1 and P_1

15 A retail price index is a direct measure of changes in:

A Average input prices paid by producers

B The prices of all goods and services produced in the economy

C The average cost of living

D Average standards of living

Answers to multiple-choice questions: Test 1

1 D	**4** C	**7** D	**10** C	**13** B
2 A	**5** C	**8** A	**11** D	**14** D
3 D	**6** B	**9** C	**12** C	**15** C

Examiner's comments

Question 1

e Answer A provides a definition of *real* national income. However, the question asks for a definition of *money* national income and not *real* national income. Money national income is real national income valued at current prices. Answer B is simply a nonsense, while C invites you to confuse flows with stocks. D is the correct answer.

Question 2

e The first statement is the only incorrect statement and so A is the answer. Point W is inside the economy's production possibility frontier so there are unemployed resources at point W. A movement from W to any point on the frontier would take up the slack in the economy or represent economic *recovery*, but true economic *growth* is best defined by an outward movement of the frontier itself. B, C and D are all correct statements. D is correct because, other things being equal, capital goods production leads to a faster rate of investment, which in turn promotes a faster growth rate.

Question 3

e Inflation involves a *decrease* in the value and purchasing power of money, so statement A is incorrect. Money national income will usually increase when inflation is taking place, but it can also increase because real national income is growing. Statement B does not therefore provide the *best* indication that inflation is taking place. A *relative* price increase means that one good has become more expensive compared to other goods. This reflects changing supply and demand conditions at the micro-level rather than inflation at the macro-level. C is therefore wrong. This leaves D as the correct answer.

Question 4

e The words 'always', 'never' and 'inevitably' should provide the clues that statements A, B and D do not provide the correct answer. The statements are too dogmatic and admit no exceptions. By contrast, the qualifying word 'may' in statement C helps identify that this is the correct answer. A higher level of aggregate demand tends to suck imports into the economy, thereby worsening the balance of payments.

Question 5

e The tax cuts mentioned in the stem of the question would expand aggregate demand but also increase rather than reduce inequalities in the distribution of income. The most likely macroeconomic objective is to reduce unemployment (answer C), since demand expansion would probably worsen both the inflation rate and the balance of payments deficit.

Question 6

Statement B is the correct answer. Whereas supply-side economists might expand aggregate demand (using monetary policy) to reduce short-term unemployment when the UK experiences recession, they believe that the most appropriate long-term policy is to improve the competitiveness and efficiency of markets. This would involve income tax cuts to promote labour market incentives.

Question 7

Statements A and C would reduce unemployment in a recession by expanding aggregate demand. Retraining schemes for redundant workers (statement C) might also be expected to reduce unemployment. This leaves D as the correct answer: an extension of employment rights would make it more costly and less attractive for employers to hire workers.

Question 8

Whereas demand-pull inflation occurs when the aggregate demand curve shifts rightward along an upward-sloping or vertical AS curve, cost-push inflation is depicted by a leftward shift of the short-run AS curve. The correct answer is therefore A.

Question 9

A cut in interest rates will increase consumption (statement A), investment (statement B) and aggregate demand (statement D). This leaves C as the correct answer. When interest rates fall, owners of funds tend to sell the pound and buy other currencies in order to earn the higher rate of return the other currencies now offer.

Question 10

Since the data are shown at constant market prices, the chart shows percentage annual changes in *real* GDP. Real GDP rose in every year except 1991. Since output of goods and services comprises real GDP, C is the correct answer. A is simply a nonsense, B is wrong for the reason just indicated, while D, although it might have happened (depending on the rate of inflation in 1991), cannot be concluded from the data.

Question 11

A, B and C are all true statements. A budget deficit must be financed by borrowing, it injects spending into the economy and it triggers a multiplier process. D, being the only untrue statement, is the answer. The budget deficit relates to fiscal policy, not monetary policy.

Question 12

An increase in wages would shift the AS curve leftward rather than rightward, while an increase in the government's budget deficit would increase aggregate demand rather than aggregate supply. A and B are therefore wrong. C is the correct answer as any event which reduces firms' costs of production causes the aggregate supply curve to shift rightward.

ultiple-choice questions

Question 13

B is the correct answer — 2000 and 2001 were two of the four years in which there was a budget surplus, with the data also showing a forecast surplus in 2005, 2006 and 2007. Statement A invites you to confuse a balance of payments deficit with a budget deficit. Statement C is wrong because the budget deficit experienced by the government would have increased rather than reduced the United States national debt. Statement D cannot be concluded from the data, though the economy almost entered recession following September 11th, 2001.

Question 14

This question tests your understanding of the relationship between short-run and long-run aggregate supply curves. The first three statements are all correct. Following an increase in aggregate demand, output can rise *temporarily* above its long-run natural level, but the short-run aggregate supply curve shifts leftward and macroeconomic equilibrium is restored at point Z. However, statement D is incorrect: the new macroeconomic equilibrium is at Z and not X. D is therefore the answer.

Question 15

Statement C provides the correct answer: a retail price index provides a measure of the cost of living. As this is not the same as the standard of living, statement D is wrong. Changes in input prices and the prices of all goods and services produced in the economy could be measured by an appropriate price index, but not by a *retail* price index which is restricted to measuring average prices of goods and services bought by consumers.

Multiple-choice questions: Test 2

1

Growth in domestic demand and real GDP
Annual % change

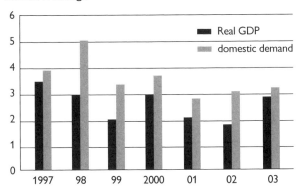

All the following statements are consistent with the data EXCEPT one. Which is the exception?

A The table shows growth in the level of real national output throughout the period 1997–2003

B Domestic demand grew faster than output and the difference may have been met by imports

C The growth in real GDP may have caused the economy's production possibility frontier to shift outwards

D The level of real GDP fell between 1998 and 1999 and the economy experienced a short recession ✓

2 Which of the following statements about economic growth is correct?

A Economic growth always improves everybody's living standard

B Negative economic growth causes the economy's production possibility frontier to shift inward ✓

C In a well-managed economy, the economy always grows at its trend growth rate

D Sustained economic growth rate completely eliminates conflict with other macro-economic policy objectives

3 Which of the following matched pairs of policy instruments and policy objectives makes most economic sense?

Policy instrument	Policy objective
A Income tax increase	Faster economic growth
B Increased government spending	Improved balance of payments
C Interest rate cut ✓	More consumption and investment
D Interest rate increase	Lower exchange rate

ultiple-choice questions

4 All the following statements about economic policy in the UK in the period 1997 to 2003 are correct EXCEPT one. Which statement is incorrect?
   A Demand-management policies were not used
   B Monetary policy was implemented by the Bank of England seeking to achieve an inflation rate target set by the government
   C Fiscal policy was used to try to create a stable macroeconomic environment
   D Supply-side policies tried to improve the efficiency and competitiveness of markets

5 An increase in the government's budget deficit is most likely to reduce:
   A Demand-deficient or cyclical unemployment
   B Demand-pull inflation
   C Structural unemployment
   D The balance of payments deficit

6 Which of the following economic conditions is likely to lead to demand-pull inflation?
   A An increase in interest rates and a rise in the world price of oil
   B An increase in government spending and firms operating at full capacity
   C Increased monopoly power in goods and labour markets
   D A worsening balance of payments deficit and a rising exchange rate

7 All the following statements relate to an increase in investment when the economy is producing on its production possibility frontier. Which statement is NOT correct?
   A In the short run, the opportunity cost of increased investment includes the production of consumer goods sacrificed
   B In the long run, the economy's production possibility frontier will probably shift outwards
   C An increase in saving may be required to finance the investment
   D The increase in investment immediately reduces demand-deficient unemployment

8 Other things being equal, an increase in the UK's balance of payments deficit means that:
   A Import prices must be falling
   B The volume of goods exported must be falling
   C Aggregate demand is falling
   D The difference between government spending and tax revenue is growing

9 The diagram opposite illustrates the aggregate supply and demand curves for an economy. The full employment level of output is y_F.

   An increase in aggregate demand from AD_1 to AD_2:
   A Could result from increased demand for imports
   B Will mean that the economy is producing on its production possibility frontier
   C Could be caused by a rise in the price of imported energy
   D Causes the purchasing power of money to fall

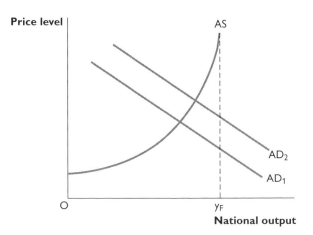

10 Which of the following is an example of fiscal policy?
  A The Bank of England imposing controls on bank lending
  B The removal of foreign exchange controls which restrict the transfer of currencies between countries
  C The removal of regulations which restrict Sunday trading
✓ D The creation of tax-exempt Individual Savings Accounts (ISAs)

11 Which of the following statements about supply-side economics is correct?
✓ A Supply-side policies are used to improve the economy's efficiency and competitiveness
  B Fiscal policy cannot be used as a part of supply-side policy
  C Supply-side economists reject the use of demand-management policies in all circumstances
  D Supply-side policies are associated with Keynesian economic policy

12 Which of the following would be most likely to reduce a balance of payments deficit?
  A Increased income tax and financial assistance for exporting industries
  B A higher exchange rate and an expansionary fiscal policy
  C An increase in the money supply and higher business taxation
✓ D A boom in the domestic economy and recession in export markets

13 The table shows how national output, prices and unemployment changed in the UK between 1997 and 1999.

| Year | Annual percentage increase | | |
	Real GDP %	Retail prices %	Unemployment %
1997	3.5	2.8	−16.5
1998	2.6	2.7	−16.0
1999	2.2	2.3	0

ultiple-choice questions

From the data it can be concluded that:

A Average living standards fell in 1998 and 1999 because the percentage increase in retail prices was greater than the increase in real GDP

B Real GDP and unemployment both grew over the 3-year period

C The long-term trend rate of growth for the UK economy is 2.76%

✓ **D** In each of the years, money national income grew by more than real national income

14 The graph below indicates the annual percentage changes in the average level of retail prices in the UK between 1976 and 2000.

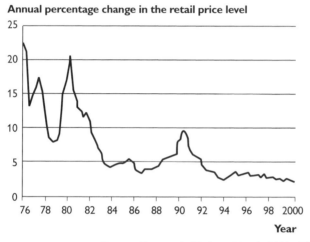

Annual percentage change in the retail price level

Year

Source: Economic Update, March 2001, Office for National Statistics.

Which of the following CANNOT be concluded from the data?

✓ **A** The value of money increased in 1991

✗ **B** The price level increased in every year between 1976 and 2000

✗ **C** Deflation of the price level did not occur during the period shown by the data

D Inflationary pressures generally fell in the UK economy over the period shown by the data

15

The United States current account balance (% GDP)

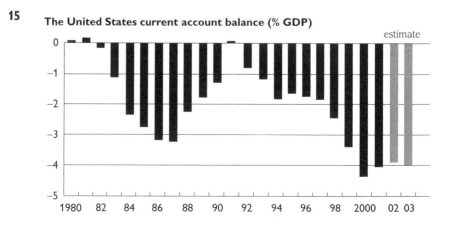

estimate

Which of the following can be inferred from the data?

X **A** US imports exceeded US exports throughout the period shown by the data

B The dollar's exchange rate fell from 1992 to 2000

X **C** The United States is a net exporter of services but a net importer of goods

✓ **D** For most of the 1990s, the United States current account was in deficit

Answers to multiple-choice questions: Test 2

1 D	**4** A	**7** D	**10** D	**13** D
2 B	**5** A	**8** C	**11** A	**14** A
3 C	**6** B	**9** D	**12** A	**15** D

Examiner's comments

Question 1

e Statements A, B and C are all consistent with the data. Statement D is the only one that is not consistent, so D is the answer. Growth was positive in all the years shown by the data, so the economy was not in recession, even though the rate of growth slowed in 1999.

Question 2

e If economic growth involves an *outward* movement of the economy's production possibility frontier, negative economic growth involves an *inward* movement. B is therefore the correct answer. The words 'always' and 'completely' in statements A, C and D help you to see that these are not correct answers.

Question 3

e C is the correct answer: lower interest rates reduce the cost of borrowing and the incentive to save, thus stimulating consumption spending by households and investment spending on capital goods by firms. The other three policy changes would produce the opposite result to that stated in the question.

Question 4

e Many students wrongly believe that since the decline of Keynesianism a generation ago, the management of aggregate demand has not figured in UK macroeconomic policy. These days, monetary policy is used to manage demand, primarily through raising or lowering interest rates so as to try and hit an inflation-rate target. *Fiscal policy* has been used to create macroeconomic stability rather than to manage demand. A is the answer.

Question 5

e A budget deficit means that government spending exceeds taxation and other sources of government revenue, thereby injecting spending and demand into the economy. The resulting increase in aggregate demand may pull up the price level and suck imports into the economy. Statements B and D are therefore wrong. A budget deficit is unlikely to have any immediate effect on structural unemployment, so C is not the answer. This leaves A as the correct answer.

Question 6

e The correct answer is B: an increase in aggregate demand in conditions of full capacity means that the price level is pulled up by excess demand. Higher interest rates (in statement A) would reduce demand-pull inflation, though initially they might raise firms' production costs. Increased monopoly power (statement C) might also trigger cost-push inflation, but not demand-pull inflation. The events specified in statement D would be deflationary.

Question 7

Statements A, B and C are all correct. Had the economy been producing initially inside rather than on its production possibility frontier, statement D would also be correct. As this is not the case, the answer is D.

Question 8

When the balance of payments is in deficit, import prices and the volume of goods exported *may* be falling (statements A and B), but neither has to be the case. However, a balance of payments deficit is *always* deflationary: it represents a leakage or withdrawal of spending from the circular flow of income. Statement C therefore provides the answer. Statement D is simply irrelevant, inviting you to confuse a balance of payments deficit with a government's budget deficit.

Question 9

The correct answer is D. According to the diagram, an increase in aggregate demand from AD_1 to AD_2 causes the price level as well as real output to rise. Whenever the price level rises, the purchasing power of money must fall. Statement A is incorrect because an increased demand for imports would reduce rather than increase aggregate demand. Since the economy is producing below the full employment level of output, it must also be inside rather than on its production possibility frontier. Hence statement B is incorrect. Lastly, a rise in the price of imported energy (statement C) would shift the AS curve leftward, though by increasing expenditure on imports it might shift the AD curve leftward as well.

Question 10

A and B are examples of monetary policy rather than fiscal policy, whilst C provides an example of deregulation or the removal of direct controls on the economy. D is an example of fiscal policy and therefore the answer: ISAs encourage households to save rather than spend on consumption because interest paid on the savings is tax exempt.

Question 11

Supply-side economists generally oppose the use of Keynesian policy, so D is wrong, but they don't reject completely the use of fiscal policy or demand management. A is the correct answer, providing a neat statement of the purpose of supply-side policy.

Question 12

Increased income tax takes demand out of the economy, thereby reducing the demand for imports. Assistance for exporting industries obviously boosts exports. Statement A therefore provides the correct answer. All the events in the other statements would tend to increase a balance of payments deficit, with the possible exception of higher business taxation in statement C. Higher business taxation could go both ways. By taking demand out of the economy, higher business taxation could reduce a payments deficit. But by reducing the international competitiveness of UK firms, it is perhaps more likely to increase a deficit.

ultiple-choice questions

Question 13

The correct answer is D: real income grew in all three years and — because inflation was also positive in all three years — money national income must have grown by more than real income. It is impossible to infer from the data that living standards fell. Statement A is therefore wrong. The data tell us that unemployment fell rather than increased, so B is also wrong. Finally, the economy grew at an average rate of 2.76% over the 3-year period, but there is insufficient data to calculate the economy's trend rate of growth.

Question 14

The graph shows the rate at which the price level increased in each year between 1976 and 2000. Inflation was positive in every year, but the rate of inflation generally fell over the whole period. Statements B, C and D are therefore correct. This leaves A as the answer: whenever inflation is positive, the value of money decreases rather than increases.

Question 15

Statement A, while true for most of the years covered by the data, was untrue in four of the years. Statements B and C cannot be inferred from the data. This leaves D as the correct answer: the United States current account was in deficit for all but four years between 1980 and 2003 (the latter, together with 2002, being a forecast deficit).

Data-response questions

Question 1

The United Kingdom economy

Total for this question: 25 marks

Study **Extracts A**, **B** and **C**, and then answer **all** parts of the question which follow.

Extract A: The United Kingdom economy 1996 to 2001

Year	GDP growth (%)	Manufacturing growth (%)	RPIX inflation (%)	Unemployment rate (%)
1996	2.6	0.4	3.0	7.0
1997	3.5	1.3	2.8	5.3
1998	2.6	0.5	2.6	4.5
1999	2.2	0.0	2.3	4.2
2000	3.0	1.7	2.1	3.6
2001	2.2	−2.3	2.1	3.2

Source: ONS *Economic Trends*.

Extract B: The UK economy in 2000

2000 was a year in which economic performance in the UK was generally satisfactory. Growth picked up, inflation remained low and unemployment fell to historically low levels.

In the past, economists have generally expected inflation to increase as unemployment falls, particularly after several years of economic growth. But in 2000, inflation   5
remained steady despite the continuing fall in the level of unemployment which appeared to put little upward pressure on wages. The underlying rate of inflation RPIX stayed consistently close to the target rate of 2.5% throughout the year. The main threat to the inflation target is no longer the possibility of the economy overheating, but rather the effects of the increase in crude oil prices and the   10
possibility of a significant exchange rate depreciation.

GDP growth was slightly higher than the long-run trend rate of growth of 2% to 2.5%. To some extent this reflects a catch-up period following the slowdown of growth in 1999. However, some economists claim that the UK has experienced a paradigm shift (a change in the structure of the economy) which has permanently increased the   15
growth rate. They argue that new information-based technologies — the 'New Economy' — have increased the trend rate of growth towards 3%. Improved use of

data-response question 1

monetary and fiscal policy to manage the economy may also have contributed to faster and more sustainable growth.

Adapted from an article in *Economic Review*, April 2001.

Extract C: The UK economy in 2001

There are worrying signs that the economic environment is deteriorating rapidly. Although the economy has survived the foot-and-mouth crisis, the situation after the terrorist attack on September 11th is potentially more serious, and may well lead to the first significant recession in the UK for 10 years. There are also serious imbalances in the economy. Consumer spending and house prices have been roaring ahead, 5 particularly in London and the southeast, while manufacturing output and investment have been falling. Sadly, the labour productivity 'miracle' hoped for a year ago appears not to have materialised.

Adapted from an article in *Economic Review*, April 2002.

(a) **Over the period from 1996 to 2001 shown in Extract A, compare the annual percentage rate of growth of manufacturing output with that of national output (GDP).** (4 marks)

(b) **Briefly explain why '…economists have generally expected inflation to increase as unemployment falls, particularly after several years of economic growth' (Extract B, lines 4–5).** (6 marks)

(c) **Drawing on the information in the data and your economic knowledge, discuss and evaluate the view expressed in Extract B that the UK economy's trend rate of growth may have increased.** (15 marks)

■ ■ ■

Candidate's answer

(a) National output measured by GDP growth grew over the whole period shown by the data. Manufacturing output grew in most years, albeit at a slower rate, but was static in 1999 and actually fell by 2.3% in 2001. The poorer performance of manufacturing output reflects its vulnerability to import competition. GDP growth was always 1% higher than the growth of manufacturing output, and in some of the years over 2% higher. This reflects the fact that services, many of which are not vulnerable to import competition, make up around 70% of GDP, whereas manufacturing output is only about 17%. Manufacturing output was in recession in 2001 (falling for over 6 months), though GDP was not in recession.

   While the answer contains sufficient comparison to earn all 4 marks, the candidate over-wrote her answer and included too much information which, though interesting and accurate, is irrelevant to the question. Although she has not lost any marks, she has penalised herself by wasting time.   **4/4 marks**

(b) Economists have generally expected inflation to increase as unemployment falls, because they are inversely related. This relationship has existed in the past and apparently the relationship has been stable, so economists have naturally expected it to continue in the future.

> ✒ This answer is not very good, earning only 1 of the available 6 marks. The first sentence does no more than state the obvious: if inflation rises as unemployment falls, there must be an inverse relationship. To earn more marks, the candidate should have provided an explanation of the relationship. For example, she might have argued that when unemployment falls, shortages of skilled labour emerge and employers bid up wages as they compete to hire scarce workers.   **1/6 marks**

(c) Extract B states that in the recent past, the UK's trend rate of growth has been 2% to 2.5% a year. The trend rate of growth is the economy's average growth rate over a long period. Mature economies in NW Europe and the US tend to have relatively low trend growth rates compared to Tiger economies and newly industrialising economies (NICs) in SE Asia. Nevertheless, when compounded, a growth rate of 2.2% enables real GDP and living standards to double every generation or so.

In the late 1990s, economists (whom I shall call optimists) argued that the trend rate of growth had increased to close to 3%. They believed that the increase was caused by the adoption of new technologies (particularly information technology) and the role of the internet in promoting new forms of economic activity such as business to business (B2B) and business to consumer (B2C). According to the optimists, these new technologies were stimulating investment and raising labour productivity (output per worker).

However, other economists (whom I shall call pessimists) challenged this view. They questioned whether the impact of ICT was sufficient to raise the economy's underlying rate of growth and argued that all that was happening was an exceptionally long upswing in the business cycle. The pessimists believe the boom will come to an end and be replaced with recession. If the next recession is as long and deep as those at the beginning of the 1980s and 1990s, the average growth rate will not have increased.

What is my view? As I write this answer Japan has entered recession, the US may just about have avoided the recession that, following the terrorist attack on September 11th, many people believed would happen, and respected economists are writing newspaper articles about the danger of contagion, i.e. the UK catching recession from the world's major economies. It is undoubtedly true that the US economy is so important to the world economy that if it suffers recession, other countries — including the UK — will suffer too. My view is that if there is a hard landing, i.e. a long and deep recession, then there is little likelihood that the trend rate of growth will have increased. However, if the next recession is short and mild (with the economy benefiting from a soft landing), it may indeed be the case that the trend rate of growth has increased.

The first paragraph, though interesting and informative, has drifted away from the set question. It should have been restricted to a definition of the trend rate of growth and statement of its percentage rate. However, the rest of the answer is excellent. It is extremely well focused, setting out one substantial new economy argument supporting the view that the trend rate of growth has increased, and another substantial argument against (relating to the possibility of recession). Most important of all, the candidate obeys the instruction to evaluate. She displays a nice overview and sufficient evaluation to take her answer into the highest Level 5 mark band (13–15 marks). Very often a good tactic to adopt when writing an evaluatory concluding paragraph is to say 'It all depends...' One set of assumptions leads to one conclusion but if the assumptions are altered, there might be a different outcome. Provided you offer some justification for your conclusion, don't be afraid to sit on the fence. **13/15 marks**

Scored 18/25   72% = grade-A/B boundary

Question 2

Consumption, saving and investment

Total for this question: 25 marks

Study **Extracts A**, **B** and **C**, and then answer **all** parts of the question which follow.

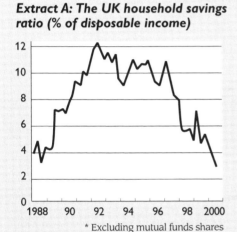

Extract A: The UK household savings ratio (% of disposable income)

* Excluding mutual funds shares

Source: *Financial Times*, 20 September 2000.

Extract B: UK personal sector real net wealth (£bn, 2000 prices)

Source: *Financial Times*, 18 November 2000.

Extract C: Consumption, not investment, drives the economy

For months, despite constant bad news, consumers have been driving the economy. High-street spending grew last month at its fastest for 3 years. This optimism may not last long. The question for economists is whether falling share prices, which have eroded wealth, could knock spending and thence damage economic growth. But it will take a lot to erode consumer confidence. Implied losses in shares have been offset   5
by continued growth in house prices. In Britain, perceptions of wealth are tied more to the fortunes of the housing market than to stocks. Property accounts for over two-thirds of total household wealth, while shares comprise only a quarter. By contrast, in the US, shares make up a much bigger proportion of wealth.

Only a minority of business sectors in the UK seem committed to the investment   10
which links directly to future national prosperity. UK investment levels are below those shown by the top international companies, in some cases markedly so. Given the growing role of technology in the production and delivery of cutting-edge products and services at a competitive price plus the greater flexibility for mass customisation

data-response question 2

this often affords, under-investment in these areas cannot bode well for the future.   15
Overall, UK companies increased investment by 10.8% in 1998. But this rate of increase
is too small to correct years of relative under-investment that has left the UK with a
capital base per employee about a third smaller than our main EU competitors and
the US, and more than 60% smaller than Japan.

Adapted from articles in the *Financial Times*, 6 December 1999 and 24 March 2001.

(a) **Compare the changes in the household savings ratio shown in Extract A with the
changes in personal sector wealth shown in Extract B over the years since 1990.**   (4 marks)

(b) **Explain how falling share prices (Extract C, line 3) may affect consumer spending
and saving in the national economy.**   (6 marks)

(c) **Making use of the data and your economic knowledge, assess the view that the
government should intervene in the national economy to promote a higher
rate of saving by households and a higher rate of investment by firms.**   (15 marks)

■ ■ ■

Candidate's answer

(a) The personal savings ratio rises in 1988 and then falls, whereas the personal
sector's wealth stays at more or less the same level in the years after 1970, but
starts rising in the late 1970s.

> Part (a) of each data-question on the national economy is likely to ask you to
> identify the main features of a table or graph or, when there are two data series
> as in this question, to compare the main changes each table or graph shows.
> This answer provides a model of bad practice when answering such a question.
> First, the candidate fails to obey the instruction to restrict comparison to the
> period after 1990. Second, he does not support his assertion of rises and falls
> in the data with any illustrative statistics drawn from the data. A good answer
> might have noted that whereas households saved 8% of disposable income in 1990,
> rising to 12% in 1992, the figure had fallen to about 3% by 2000. Meanwhile,
> personal wealth more than doubled in real terms over the period, from around
> £1,000 billion in 1990 to over £2,000 billion in 2000. Because of these omissions,
> the answer earned only 1 of the available 4 marks.   **1/4 marks**

(b) As the passage states: 'Falling share prices erode wealth and knock consumer
spending.' People who hold a substantial part of their wealth in shares become
considerably less wealthy when share prices fall significantly. They are likely to
spend less and save more for two main reasons. First, they save more to 'top up'
or restore their eroded wealth to its previous value. Second, they save more
because they feel less confident about the future, a 'feel bad' factor having replaced
the previous 'feel good' factor.

✎ This is an excellent answer, introducing and then explaining two points sufficiently to earn full marks. **6/6 marks**

(c) Extract A shows the personal saving ratio in the UK falling to around 3% in 2000. Likewise, Extract C indicates that the rate of investment by firms in the UK is below that of our main international competitors. It can be argued that the UK's relatively poor economic performance stretching back over decades is partly due to a low rate of investment. Also, it is sometimes argued that because we save too little, we consume too much and that the resulting excess demand causes inflation and balance of payments problems when the excess demand is spent on imports.

There is, therefore, a case for the government intervening to promote higher savings and investment to get us into line with our main international competitors. The government already does this to some extent through the tax system. Previous Conservative governments created the Tax Exempt Saving Scheme (TESSA) and Personal Equity Plans (PEPs) to give tax advantages to saving. More recently, the Labour government replaced these with Individual Savings Accounts (ISAs). Likewise, businesses can offset spending on investment in new capital equipment against tax.

But clearly tax advantages on their own are not enough to increase savings and investment to an appropriate level. There is a case for the government undertaking more active policies, especially with regard to investment. Here, the main thing the government could do is to grant financial assistance or subsidies to firms, e.g. £1 of government money for every £2 invested by a firm. This used to be done on a significant level with Regional Development Grants as a part of regional policy. It is less clear how governments could promote saving, other than through tax advantages. Compulsion or forcing people to save would clearly be out of order. Perhaps a return to advertising National Saving as being a patriotic duty would work. One policy to encourage saving currently being used relates to the running down of the state retirement pension. Unless they are prepared to live eventually in poverty, many people must now contribute to a stakeholder pension. This is a form of saving.

Overall, there is a case for the government promoting saving and investment, but it must be done with caution. Current rates of saving and investment represent a form of market failure, but the wrong type of government intervention might lead instead to government failure.

✎ This is a Level 4 answer because two or more relevant issues are recognised, there is a reasonable attempt to apply economic concepts and ideas, alternative points of view are recognised, and there is *some* attempt to evaluate issues and arguments. (Level 4 covers the mark range 10–12.) However, there is not enough economic analysis or evaluation to reach the highest Level 5. The two main ways in which the answer could be improved are: (i) identification and then analysis of the case against government intervention; and (ii) fuller evaluation which develops the market failure versus government failure distinction. (The latter shows a relevant use of concepts

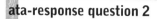

learned when studying Module I: Markets and Market Failure.) With regard to the first point, the candidate might have discussed issues such as the opportunity cost of government intervention, e.g. subsidies might mean higher taxes or reduced government spending on hospitals, schools etc. He might also have drawn on the point made in Extract C that investment may sometimes be inefficient. In the past, there is some evidence (such as the regional policy which the candidate mentions) that instead of picking winners, government subsidy of firms leads to the propping up of losers. **10/15 marks**

Scored 17/25 **68% = grade B**

Question 3

Monetary and fiscal policy

Total for this question: 25 marks

Study **Extracts A** and **B**, and then answer **all** parts of the question which follow.

Extract A: Monetary and fiscal policy under New Labour

Immediately on coming to power in 1997, the Labour government reformed the framework within which monetary policy is conducted. The Bank of England was made operationally independent, with the then newly-created Monetary Policy Committee responsible for implementing policy to achieve the 2.5% inflation rate target set by the government. Two years later, the government introduced a new fiscal policy framework to meet the two key requirements that: 5

(i) fiscal policy should deliver sound public finances and thus prevent government itself being a source of adverse shocks on the economy;

(ii) by promoting stability, fiscal policy should play an important role in supporting monetary policy. 10

A new Code for Fiscal Stability provided the framework for the government's fiscal policy based on the five principles of transparency, stability, responsibility, fairness and efficiency. It has given rise to two strict fiscal rules which provide the means to deliver sound public finances. These are:

(i) The golden rule which says that on average over the economic or business cycle, 15 the government will borrow only to invest and not to finance current spending. The government can borrow without having to repay the debt within the span of the business cycle only if the borrowing finances the acquisition of capital assets. This is because capital spending generates assets that confer benefits to both current and future generations. 20

(ii) The sustainable investment rule which says that public sector net debt as a proportion of GDP will be held over the economic cycle at a stable and prudent level. This is because high levels of public debt can reduce the government's ability to buffer the economy against major shocks and because debt may impose other costs such as the higher interest rates which reduce business investment. 25

Fiscal policy is now based on meeting these two fiscal policy rules rather than on discretionary changes in tax rates and levels of public spending in order to manage demand. The government's aim is to create a stable and predictable fiscal environment in which changes in taxation and public spending are announced well in advance of the actual introduction of the changes, thereby enabling economic agents in the 30 private sector, particularly businesses, to plan for the future in conditions of certainty.

Adapted from the Treasury's *Red Book*, 1999 Budget.

data-response question 3

Extract B: Taxes and public spending (% GDP)

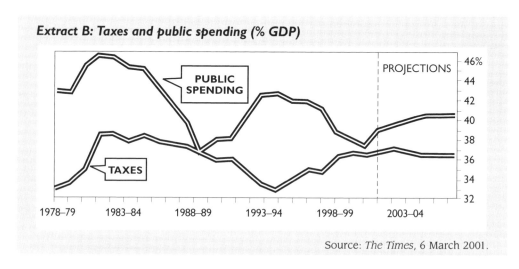

Source: *The Times*, 6 March 2001.

(a) **Compare the changes in taxes and public spending as percentages of GDP over the period from 1978 to 2001 which are shown in Extract B.** (4 marks)

(b) **Explain *two* ways in which a fall in taxation as a percentage of GDP may affect the national economy.** (6 marks)

(c) **Do you agree that monetary policy and fiscal policy should be used in the ways indicated in Extract A? Justify your reasoning.** (15 marks)

■ ■ ■

Candidate's answer

(a) It is important to note that both taxes and public spending in Extract B are shown as proportions of GDP (national output) and not as absolute levels. Over the period 1978 to 1988, there was a positive correlation between the two data series, both increasing as proportions of GDP until 1983, then both decreasing. However, public spending was absorbing a much greater proportion of GDP. This implies the existence of a budget deficit during this period, but the two came together in 1998 so maybe the budget was balanced. For virtually all the rest of the period up to 2001, the two data series were negatively correlated. The percentage of national income absorbed by public spending grew until 1993, while taxation as a per cent fell, but the opposite was true for most of the rest of the period until 2001.

e This answer earns 3 of the available 4 marks. There are three good points in the answer, namely a clear understanding of the meaning of the two data series, the recognition of correlations and the linkage of the two data series to the state of the government's budget. However, to earn full marks she needed to quote a few representative statistics, e.g. public spending ranging from a high of over 46% of GDP to a low of about 37%, while taxes varied between 33% and 39% of GDP.

3/4 marks

(b) The two ways I shall explain relate to aggregate demand and to supply-side incentives. I shall illustrate both with an AD/AS diagram:

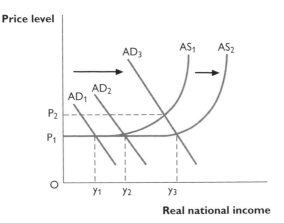

A fall in taxation as a percentage of GDP will lead to an injection of spending into the circular flow of income. This will increase aggregate demand and lead to a multiplier effect whereby national income increases by more than the initial increase in aggregate demand. If initially there was plenty of spare capacity, real output and employment would grow. However, if the economy started off at full capacity, excess demand might pull up the price level. In the former case the AD curve in my diagram might shift from AD_1 to AD_2; in the latter case from AD_2 to AD_3. By contrast, if the main effect of the fall in taxation, e.g. through income tax cuts, was to increase labour market incentives, the AS curve in my diagram would shift rightward from AS_1 to AS_2, increasing the economy's productive capacity.

🖉 This is an excellent answer earning full marks. However, as the next answer shows, the candidate has spent too much time answering parts (a) and (b). As a result, the quality of her answer to part (c) suffers. **6/6 marks**

(c) Extract A indicates that monetary policy is currently used in the UK as a part of counter-inflation policy. The government sets a 2.5% inflation rate target and then instructs the Bank of England's Monetary Policy Committee (MPC) to implement monetary policy by raising or lowering interest rates, so as to achieve the target. Under New Labour, the Bank would have to cut interest rates if actual inflation fell below 2.5%, as well as raise interest rates if inflation ends up above 2.5%. The Bank has been very successful in achieving the 2.5% target since 1997, so — the proof of the pudding being in the eating — this is evidence of the policy's success.

As the passage also says, fiscal policy is implemented by the Treasury and not by the Bank of England and is used to create macroeconomic stability. The Treasury does this by raising or lowering taxes and public spending and by abiding by the two fiscal policy rules outlined in the extract.

data-response question 3

I believe both policies should be used in the ways indicated in the extract, though if I was a Conservative I might disagree. Unfortunately I haven't got time to explain fully my reasoning, but one justification is that it represents an efficient division of labour between the Treasury and the Bank of England.

e After the quality of her earlier work, this is a disappointing answer. The candidate achieves Level 3 (7–9 marks) because she makes some attempt to evaluate the track record of monetary policy. Her only point is that the use of monetary policy is justified by its success in hitting the 2.5% target. However, she wastes too much of the limited time at her disposal by, for the most part, restricting her answer to describing monetary and fiscal policy. This is unnecessary because Extract A already provides the description. Her coverage of fiscal policy is very thin. She includes a proverb and cracks a joke as well. There is no harm in this and it enlivens her answer, but beware of upsetting examiners who may not take kindly to an adolescent polemic. And remember, the person who marks your script may have opposite views to your own. On balance, this was a missed opportunity. The candidate's earlier answers suggested she could have achieved a high grade A, but she failed to deliver. **8/15 marks**

Scored 17/25   **68% = grade B**

Question 4

Unemployment and inflation

Total for this question: 25 marks

Study **Extracts A**, **B** and **C**, and then answer **all** parts of the question which follow.

	Unemployment rate	Inflation rate
1992	9.7	4.7
1993	10.3	3.0
1994	9.6	2.3
1995	8.6	2.9
1996	8.2	3.0
1997	7.1	2.8
1998	6.1	2.6
1999	6.0	2.3
2000	5.5	2.1
2001	5.2	1.9

Extract A:
UK unemployment as a percentage of the economically active population (ILO measure), and the headline rate of inflation (measured by RPI), 1992–2001

Source: *Annual Abstract of Statistics*, 2001 edition.

Extract B: Tight labour market leaves many employers trawling for workers

UK unemployment, measured by the claimant count, is likely to fall this month below 1 million for the first time in 25 years. And unfilled vacancies, which indicate the extent to which unemployment is frictional, have hit a record high. Richard Jeffrey, an economist at ING Charterhouse Securities, warns: 'Unemployment has fallen much further than many people would have thought possible. The more it falls the nearer we get to the point where earnings really start to take off.' If that happens, he says, employers will have to pass higher costs on to consumers by raising prices, in which case cost-push inflation will occur or endanger long-term prospects by cutting investment.

Adapted from an article in the *Financial Times*, 14 March 2001.

Extract C: Why has unemployment fallen?

The recent reduction in unemployment may be the result of a structural improvement in the labour market, or it may be simply the result of a cyclical upturn in the economy.

data-response question 4

An expansion in demand which runs ahead of the economy's productive potential will in due course lead to inflation. Economists call this demand-pull inflation. As there has not been much inflation in recent years, a large part of the reduction in unemployment could be associated with a structural improvement in the labour market and should therefore be sustainable. UK governments have claimed that supply-side policies have been responsible for much of the structural improvement in the labour market and the fall in unemployment.

5

Adapted from an article in *Economic Review*, February 1998.

(a) Compare the changes shown in Extract A which occurred in the UK unemployment and inflation rates over the period 1992–2001. (4 marks)

(b) Explain how, according to the data, inflation may be caused in the UK economy. (6 marks)

(c) Indicate how aggregate demand may be managed to reduce unemployment, and discuss whether this is the most appropriate way to reduce unemployment in the UK today. (15 marks)

■ ■ ■

Candidate's answer

(a) The unemployment rate was 9.7% in 1992. It then rose, peaking at 10.3% in 1993, before falling continuously over the rest of the years, dropping to 5.2% in 2001. Inflation fell more or less continuously over the 10 year period.

e While you must resist the temptation simply to write a year-by-year account of changes in the unemployment and inflation rates, to gain full marks it is necessary to quote rather more statistics than the candidate has done in this case. He has detected the trends for both unemployment and inflation, but his comparison is implicit rather than explicit. A simple statement that both unemployment and inflation were moving downward over the decade, but that small increases in the inflation rate in 1995 and 1996 were offset by a fall in 1997 would pick up 2 more marks. A mark could also be earned by calculating the overall percentage changes in the unemployment and inflation rates over the period. **2/4 marks**

(b) Economists use two types of theory to explain inflation: demand theories and cost theories. With the former, an expansion of aggregate demand creates excess demand, assuming that the economy is at or close to full capacity, in which case the aggregate supply of output is inelastic and cannot be increased to meet demand. The excess demand pulls up the price level. The monetarist theory of inflation is a demand-pull theory. According to this theory, the government allows excess money to be created, which, when spent, pulls up the price level. By contrast, cost inflation relates to firms passing on as price increases any increase they suffer in costs of production. The cost increase could be caused by wages rising faster than labour productivity, or by increased raw material or energy costs.

✐ This answer provides a classic example of a candidate with plenty of knowledge failing to score a high mark because he has not answered the set question. Key words in the question are 'according to the data'. By ignoring this instruction, the candidate has restricted himself to half marks, despite his good understanding of theories and possible causes of inflation. **3/6 marks**

(c) Aggregate demand is the total planned expenditure upon national output exercised by all the economic agents in the economy. It comprises consumption, investment, government spending net of taxation, and exports minus imports. The management of aggregate demand refers to the use of monetary policy, and possibly fiscal policy, by the government to shift the economy's aggregate demand curve rightward or leftward. If the government wants to manage aggregate demand to reduce unemployment, it will try to shift the AD curve rightwards. It could do this with an expansionary fiscal policy or an expansionary monetary policy. With the former, the government cuts taxes or increases government spending (either of which might create or enlarge a budget deficit, injecting spending into the circular flow of income). By contrast, with monetary policy the government — or rather the Bank of England these days — cuts interest rates, thereby stimulating consumption and investment. The resulting rightward shift of the AD curve is shown below. Real national income or output rises from y_1 to y_2. Unemployment falls because more workers are hired to produce the extra output.

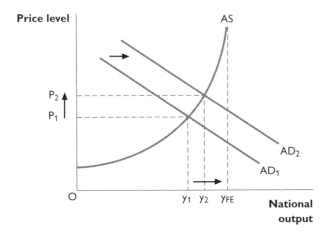

Managing aggregate demand to reduce unemployment is the most appropriate method of reducing unemployment — provided national output in the UK economy today is below the full employment level of output (y_{FE} in the diagram). Unemployment fell steadily during most of the 1990s (as Extract A shows) and fell

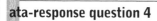

ata-response question 4

below 1 million in 2001. If national output is still below the full employment level, then expanding aggregate demand through interest rate cuts is the most appropriate way of reducing unemployment in the UK today.

e Again, the answer is ultimately disappointing despite the candidate's excellent knowledge. The main problem is lack of balance between the two parts of the question. The candidate has written more than enough on the first part but has failed to get to grips with the second, more demanding, part of the question which required significantly more evaluation or assessment. He might have explained that, as his diagram shows, an expansion of aggregate demand inflates the price level as well as reflating real output and employment. He might also have discussed various types or causes of unemployment. Expanding aggregate demand is appropriate for reducing demand-deficient (or cyclical) unemployment, but it is inappropriate if UK unemployment has other causes. Arguably, supply-side policies are the most appropriate policies for increasing employment, and reducing unemployment, in the long run. **11/15 marks**

Scored 16/25   64% = grade-B/C boundary

Question 5

The UK's productivity gap

Total for this question: 25 marks

Study **Extracts A**, **B**, **C** and **D**, and then answer **all** parts of the question which follow.

	UK	France	Germany	Japan	US
Whole economy	2.2	2.8	2.6	3.1	0.8
Marketed sectors	2.6	2.9	2.7	3.1	1.2

Extract A: Average annual percentage growth rates of labour productivity for selected countries, 1973–95

	UK	France	Germany	Japan	US
1973	100	110	126	71	175
1979	100	123	140	74	160
1996	100	120	131	81	128

Extract B: Index numbers of levels of labour productivity for selected countries (UK =100)

Extract C: Productivity in the United Kingdom

Productivity is defined as the amount of output produced per unit of input. It comes in different forms. The one most commonly discussed in the media is labour productivity.

It is often claimed that Britain has a 'productivity problem' or 'productivity gap' compared to countries with which the UK competes. It is said that Britain has 5 performed poorly compared with a number of other countries in terms of both the level of labour productivity and its rate of growth.

Adapted from an article in *Economic Review*, February 2000.

Extract D: Productivity and growth

Long-term economic growth depends on a number of factors. One of these is the rate of productivity growth. The government recently announced its ambition to drive the UK's productivity growth rate above is competitors. This is no small ambition, given that the US has been enjoying a technology-based spurt in productivity up 2.5% a year since 1996. But most analysis suggests that the UK's improved productivity 5

ata-response question 5

performance in the 1990s had more to do with supply-side reforms of its labour market rather than a US-style leap into the new economy.

Adapted from an article in the *Independent*, 20 November 2000.

(a) **Compare the changes of labour productivity in the United Kingdom and its competitor countries, which are shown in Extracts A and B.** (4 marks)

(b) **Explain why a productivity gap may pose problems for the UK economy.** (6 marks)

(c) **Drawing on the data and on your economic knowledge, identify various factors which might contribute to an increase in labour productivity in the UK in future years, and evaluate the significance of the factors you identify.** (20 marks)

■ ■ ■

Candidate's answer

(a) Extract A shows that UK labour productivity increased in every year between 1973 and 1995, but that the rate of increase was slower than in the other countries shown except the US. This information conflicts with that shown in Extract B. Here UK productivity remains constant at 100 in each of the three years shown. According to Extract B, US performance was worse than that of the UK: productivity actually fell in the US.

e This answer displays a poor understanding of two of the main ways in which data are likely to be presented in your exam: percentage rates of growth and index numbers. Nevertheless, the candidate picks up 2 of the 4 marks by stating that labour productivity increased and that the rate of increase was lower than in competitor countries. He made basic omissions and mistakes in data interpretation but, because answers are marked *positively* rather than *negatively*, marks are not deducted for mistakes, however naïve. The data show *average* productivity increases over the whole of the data period, but the candidate asserted that productivity increased in *every* year. Second, he failed to quote any of the statistics as evidence. Third, the last part of his answer is nonsense. Extract B permits comparison of productivity levels for the six countries shown for *each* of the three years, but not a comparison of changes in productivity *across* the three years.

2/4 marks

(b) The main reason why a productivity gap may pose problems for the UK economy relates to deteriorating competitiveness. Britain's economy will become increasingly uncompetitive if the productivity gap persists or widens. A second reason is that low productivity means that national income and living standards are lower than they could be. The population may become dissatisfied and cause trouble for the government.

e The candidate identifies two reasons why a productivity gap may pose problems for the government, but fails to explain or develop either of the points. This restricts his score to a mark for each point, the first point made being the strongest. It is insufficient to assert that competitiveness will deteriorate. Competitiveness (or uncompetitiveness) must be defined and the answer must then explain why deteriorating competitiveness may pose problems for the economy (e.g. deteriorating price and/or quality competitiveness makes UK exports less attractive in overseas markets and imports more attractive in the UK market). The candidate's second point could be expanded by explaining that the purpose of economic activity is to improve economic welfare and human happiness. A relatively low level of output or income per capita means that people are less well-off in material terms than the inhabitants of competitor countries. Low productivity poses a problem for a government aiming to maximise economic growth and welfare.   **2/6 marks**

(c) Labour productivity can increase if (i) people work harder; (ii) workers' motivation increases; (iii) workers become more skilled; (iv) the quantity of capital (machinery etc.) per worker increases; and (v) the quality of capital improves, incorporating the latest technical progress.

I believe that the last two of the factors I have listed are most significant, together with a further factor: the efficiency with which production is organised. For example, a modern car factory such as Nissan's at Sunderland achieves much higher labour productivity than Rover's Longbridge factory because it is designed so that modern methods of production — based on the just-in-time principle and Japanese production methods — can be implemented. By contrast, Longbridge suffers from old buildings and an inefficient factory layout.

The first method of increasing labour productivity that I have mentioned can be called the 'blood, sweat and tears' method. Driving workers to work harder can improve productivity in the short run, but it will suffer from the impact of the law of diminishing returns in the long run and workers' motivation may also be adversely affected.

e This is an interesting answer with some good points, but it lacks sufficient explanation and discussion of the points made. The style of the answer shows that the candidate has drawn (relevantly) on knowledge and understanding picked up from the business and finance pages of newspapers, or possibly from a business studies course. It is all good stuff and certainly shows some evaluation. Overall, the answer reached a Level 4 (10–12 marks). To reach Level 5, the candidate would have to develop the points he makes, such as just-in-time production and the impact of the law of diminishing returns. This predicts that as more workers are added to fixed productive capacity, the benefits of specialisation and the division of labour become exhausted and eventually the extra output (or marginal product) produced by an extra worker begins to fall. Perhaps the most important concept which would benefit from further discussion is investment. Two types of investment are relevant: investment in physical capital (machinery and other capital goods) and investment in human capital (training and developing the skills of workers). The former involves providing workers with more capital and better

data-response question 5

capital or state-of-the-art machinery which is the end product of technical progress and innovation. Although the candidate did mention this, he needed to develop his answer beyond a brief statement.   **11/15 marks**

Scored 15/25   60% = grade C

Question 6

The threat of recession

Total for this question: 25 marks

Study **Extracts A**, **B**, **C** and **D**, and then answer **all** parts of the question which follow.

Extract A: Household consumption, £bn, 1995 prices

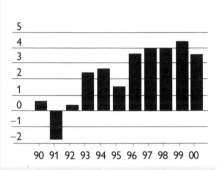

Source: *Guardian*, 4 April 2001.

Extract B: Balance of trade, £bn

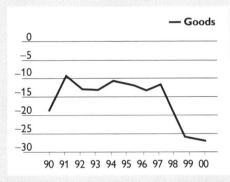

Source: *Guardian*, 4 April 2001.

Extract C: Britain starts to wobble

Is the UK about to be pulled under by a world recession? If the negative forces now building up prove to be as dangerous as some fear, it will take more than a few cuts in interest rates by the Bank of England's Monetary Policy Committee to keep the UK economy afloat.

Industrial production fell 0.3% in February and is being damaged by the downturn   5
in the US. Overall output was down 0.7% in the latest 3 months. If this continues, the UK economy will soon officially be in recession. In the US a sharp slowdown has coincided with renewed difficulties in Japan and an easing of growth in Euroland. The spectre is of the first synchronised slowdown and recession in the three leading economic regions of the world in the modern era. Growing inter-dependence may mean   10
that in the modern era everybody sinks or swims together.

Adapted from an article in the *Sunday Times*, 8 April 2001.

Extract D: Will there be a balance of payments problem?

There is a deep problem in the British economy — the tendency for spending to out-strip the increase in productive capacity. Over the past 5 years, household spending

ata-response question 6

has increased by 4% a year on average, and of the 2.8% average growth in GDP over that period, 2.5% has come from household consumption. The growth in domestic demand led by consumption spending has far outstripped the economy's ability to supply. 5

For decades, that tendency to spend more than the nation produces has been flagged by the imbalance between demand and supply showing up in the current account of the balance of payments. The portents here are not good. The current account is now feeling the full impact of the over-valuation of sterling, which makes 10 exports dearer and imports cheaper. A strong pound, the absence of foreign tourists, falling US demand and slower global growth suggest that at some point in the not-too-distant future the age-old problem of the balance of payments will again rear its head.

Adapted from an article in the Guardian *4 April, 2001.*

(a) **For the period 1990–2000, compare the changes in household consumption and the changes in balance of trade, which are shown in Extracts A and B.** (4 marks)

(b) **Explain why a 'synchronised slowdown and recession in the three leading economic regions of the world' (Extract C, lines 9–10) may make it more difficult for the UK to use economic policy to bring the national economy out of recession.** (6 marks)

(c) **Do you agree with the view expressed in lines 11–14 of Extract D that, in the not-too-distant future, the balance of payments may pose significant problems for the UK economy? Justify your reasoning.** (15 marks)

■ ■ ■

Candidate's answer

(a) I can detect an inverse or negative relationship between household consumption and the balance of trade. This means that as consumption grows, the trade deficit deteriorates. An important point to note about the balance of trade (the value of goods exported minus the value of goods imported) is that it is in deficit throughout the period. When consumption fell by over £2 billion from 1990 to 1991, the trade deficit also fell, i.e. improved by about £10 billion. For most of the rest of the period (except 1995 and 2000), consumption grew. The trade deficit remained more or less constant until 1997, fluctuating between £10 billion and £13 billion (i.e. there was not much of a relationship), but the deficit then increased rapidly to £27 billion in 2001.

> *The candidate has written an excellent answer which displays a confident understanding of the data. He has resisted the temptation to write about causes of the relationship between consumption and the balance of payments, but the way he has written the answer indicates that he could have provided such an explanation had it been required.* **4/4 marks**

(b) The UK is only a small part of the world economy, but it is what economists call an open economy which means it is open to trade with the rest of the world. Changes in exports and imports can affect the UK economy for better or for worse without the British government having the power to do anything about this.

> In contrast to his earlier answer, the candidate fails to develop his answer suffi-
> ciently to score more than half marks. Synchronised recessions would cause
> export markets to collapse and foreign direct investment (FDI) into the UK to
> dry up. In 2001 many economists feared this was happening. The US, Japan and
> possibly Euroland appeared to be entering recession together, especially after the
> terrorist attack on September 11th, 2001. Through a contagion process, the UK
> might be dragged into deep recession, suffering a hard landing rather than the
> relatively mild discomfort of a soft landing. **3/6 marks**

(c) The writer of Extract D implies that the trade deficit shown in Extract B will get worse because of (i) a high and overvalued exchange rate which makes the UK's exports uncompetitive and imports too competitive; (ii) falling demand in the rest of the world resulting from the state of economies overseas; and (iii) one-off adverse effects or shocks such as foreign tourists being scared off by the foot and mouth epidemic affecting farm animals in 2001.

Assuming the balance of payments deteriorates as forecast in Extract B, will this pose significant problems for the UK economy? As is often the case in economics, the answer is 'it all depends'. It may pose a problem if it signals price and quality uncompetitiveness of UK goods and services in world markets. This could trigger further deindustrialisation (the decline of industries, particularly manufacturing industries) and the return of growing unemployment. It could also pose a problem if the government wishes to maintain a high or strong exchange rate. A growing trade deficit usually makes it difficult to do this. This would pose the greatest problem if the UK wished to stabilise the exchange rate at a high level in advance of joining the single currency or euro.

However, most commentators agree that joining the euro at a high exchange rate would build permanent international uncompetitiveness into the UK economy. Therefore a fall in the exchange rate caused by a balance of payments deficit could be a good thing. Related to this, if the exchange rate continues to float and to be determined by the forces of supply and demand, a growing balance of payments deficit should cause the exchange rate to fall, and as a result the price competitiveness of UK exports will be restored.

Even this would not be the end of the story. A falling exchange rate, caused by a balance of payments deficit, may then raise the UK's inflation rate. This is because a falling exchange rate increases the price of imported food, energy, raw materials and consumer goods. Higher inflation would then make UK goods more expensive and less competitive than imports. This would further worsen the balance of payments. A vicious downward spiral of another fall in the exchange rate, further inflation, eroded competitiveness and a further deterioration of the exchange rate might ensue.

In conclusion, the balance of payments may well provide significant problems for the UK economy in the future. However, I wish to make three qualifications to

my conclusion. First, the balance of payments has been in record deficit in the recent past, without a repeat of the balance of payments crises of 30 years ago. The absence of crises may continue. Second, if the UK economy suffers recession, as Extract C warns, fewer imports will be drawn into the UK economy so, in this circumstance, the balance of payments should improve. Third, if the pound joins the euro, pressure can no longer be imposed on the pound's exchange rate for the simple reason that the pound will no longer exist.

This is a model part (c) answer. The candidate identifies, discusses and evaluates both sides of the issue posed by the question. The answer is nicely structured, well balanced and has a well-argued conclusion. As the question requires, the candidate's reasoning is fully justified.   **15/15 marks**

Scored 22/25   88% = high grade A